Joachim Klang

LEGO TIPS FOR KIDS
space

HEEL

ACKNOWLEDGMENTS

Thanks to some pioneers and revolutionaries, some of whom we know in person and admire:

2LegoOrNot2Lego	- Derfel Cadarn -	Karwik	McBricker	Spencer_R
Arvo Brothers	Digger1221	Lazer Blade	Mijasper	T.Oechsner
ArzLan	Eastpole77	lego_nabii	Misterzumbi	Taz-Maniac
Bart Willen	Fianat	Legohaulic	Nannan Z	ted @ndes
Brian Corredor	Fraslund	LEGOLAS	NENN	TheBrickAvenger
Bricksonwheels	Fredoichi	Legonardo Davidy	Obedient Machine	Théolego
Brickthing	Gabe Umland	Legopard	Ochre Jelly	tnickolaus
Bricktrix	Gambort	Legotrucks	„Orion Pax"	Toltomeja
Bruceywan	gearcs	_lichtblau_	Paul Vermeesch	x_Speed
captainsmog	Henrik Hoexbroe	‚LL'	Pepa Quin	Xenomurphy
Cole Blaq	Homa	Mark of Falworth	RoccoB	
Cuahchic	Joe Meno	markus19840420	Sir Nadroj	
DecoJim	Jojo	marshal banana	Sirens-Of-Titan	

Special thanks go to Manny Jasus (Obedient Machine) for his wonderful inspiration and for permitting the use of his creations. You can visit him at www.Flickr.com.
A huge thank-you likewise to Uwe Kurth for his brilliant rendering of the Viper.

HEEL Verlag GmbH
Gut Pottscheidt
53639 Königswinter
Germany
Tel.: +49 (0) 2223 9230-0
Fax: +49 (0) 2223 9230-13
E-Mail: info@heel-verlag.de
www.heel-verlag.de

© 2016 HEEL Verlag GmbH

Author: Joachim Klang
Layout, Design, and Illustration: Odenthal Illustration, www.odenthal-illustration.de
Photography: Jennifer Zumbusch, www.zumbusch-fotografie.de
Translated from German by: Susan Ghanouni in association with First Edition Translations Ltd, Cambridge, UK
Edited by: Robert Anderson in association with First Edition Translations Ltd, Cambridge, UK
Project management: Ulrike Reihn-Hamburger

ISBN 978-3-95843-390-8

CONTENT

THE AUTHOR

This is Joe. You may already have encountered Joe, who goes under the nickname of -derjoe-, in other contexts but his real passion is reserved for LEGO's colorful building bricks.

Joe will guide you through this book in his usual way and help you with tips and hints whenever things get a little complicated.

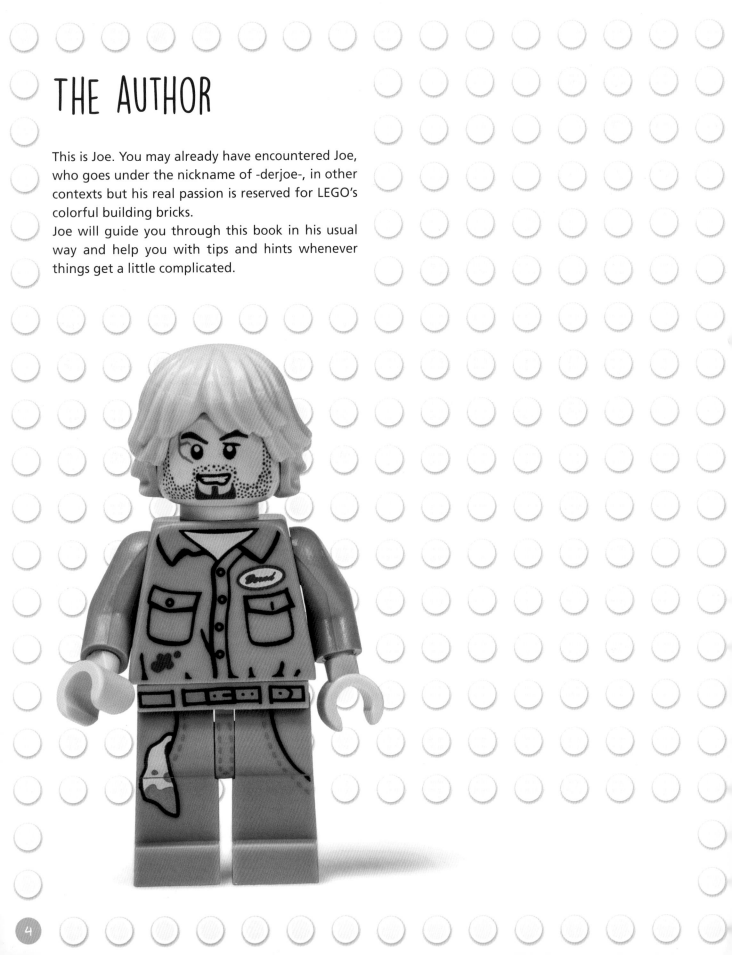

FOREWORD

The idea behind my new book, which is specifically aimed at younger fans of this colorful construction toy, is to create cool spaceships, robots, and characters from our favorite sci-fi movies and TV shows from as few pieces as possible.

It goes without saying that the contents of individual LEGO collections will vary considerably, depending very much on which sets you have bought or been given in the past. I myself always try to find the perfect solution by choosing pieces that are best suited to the purpose. I am obviously thoroughly familiar with which bricks are available in which colors in the LEGO range and also know which of these I have in my own collection or are available for purchase. I can only make a rough guess at which bricks you might have in your own LEGO box. You may find, therefore, that your collection does not include a particular brick that I have used in my models. Some of you, on the other hand, may have large quantities of pieces that I myself have had to order specially.

You may well find that you cannot immediately get started on building the model you have chosen from this book. But please do not be put off! Try to find an alternative for the missing piece and be creative.

One of your friends may well have a duplicate of the piece you need. Or you might find it included in a small set in your neighborhood store. If not, you can always order the piece in question on the Internet, e.g. through eBay or BrickLink. Or else you could buy it from LEGOLAND, any LEGO store, or the LEGO online store. I am always finding useful pieces at flea markets or various LEGO trading platforms. Each model is followed by a list of required pieces, which clearly specifies each of the elements used. The fact that there are over 38,000 different types of LEGO pieces makes this hobby of ours incredibly versatile and may even encourage you to become a LEGO hunter or collector in your own right.

The models in this book will hopefully inspire and encourage you to create models of your own. Using the ones I have created and described in this book, I would like to show you a few construction techniques and ideas, which, with a little imagination, can be used as the basis to create some excellent models of your own. When it comes to LEGO, you can build absolutely anything!

Enjoy!

THE WONDERFUL DIVERSITY OF LEGO ELEMENTS

There is a huge variety of different building elements in the LEGO range. By early 2016 a LEGO builder could choose from over 38,000 pieces in all shapes and sizes—available in a range of over 150 colors. This allows for a vast number of combination possibilities.

Even so, revolutionary new bricks keep on appearing, facilitating the development of brand-new construction techniques. If you are like me and have a long history of building and experimenting with LEGO, you will have your own list of favorite pieces. At the moment, my particular favorites are the following:

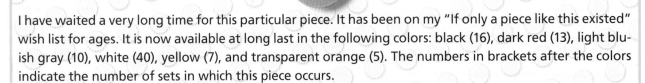

85861 Plate, Round 1 x 1 with Open Stud

I have waited a very long time for this particular piece. It has been on my "If only a piece like this existed" wish list for ages. It is now available at long last in the following colors: black (16), dark red (13), light bluish gray (10), white (40), yellow (7), and transparent orange (5). The numbers in brackets after the colors indicate the number of sets in which this piece occurs.

The hole in the center of the plate is exactly the same size as the hand of a minifigure, thereby opening up a whole range of options for use. I have used it in several models in this book since most of my constructions here are small-scale.

4697b Pneumatic T Piece New Style (T Bar)

This element has been around for a while but it has only recently become available in black. The dark color means that it can be incorporated in a model very unobtrusively. I used T bars for joints in the Han Solo figure, for example.

11203 Tile, Modified 2 x 2 Inverted

The special feature of this tile is that it is inverted on the inside, opening up all kinds of new possibilities. This element, eagerly awaited by LEGO fans all over the world, is also available in a whole range of colors: black (3), bright pink (3), dark gray (63), light bluish gray (2), magenta (1), tan (20), and white (13). The numbers in brackets once again indicate the number of sets that include this particular color. I used this tile when making the figure of Han Solo, our favorite smuggler.

BUILDING MADE SIMPLE

Everything in this book is intended to be as simple as possible. However, what one person may find easy may well be too difficult for someone else. That is why this book—like my other books—is structured according to increasing levels of difficulty. We begin with these figures constructed from 2x2 bricks, plates, and tiles. They may not have arms or faces but the individual figures are nevertheless instantly recognizable. Assuming, of course, that you are familiar with the original characters.

WALL—E

This friendly little fellow captured our hearts in a big way with his quest to find his beloved Eve. I wanted to give my model the same ability to convey his feelings entirely through his binocular eyes. I therefore used a ball joint for the neck in order to allow the head as much movement as possible. Have a look through the next few pages yourself and try to guess which emotion the robot is conveying in each case. Unfortunately, with a model of this size, the tracks are not movable but I obviously had to give him something along those lines.

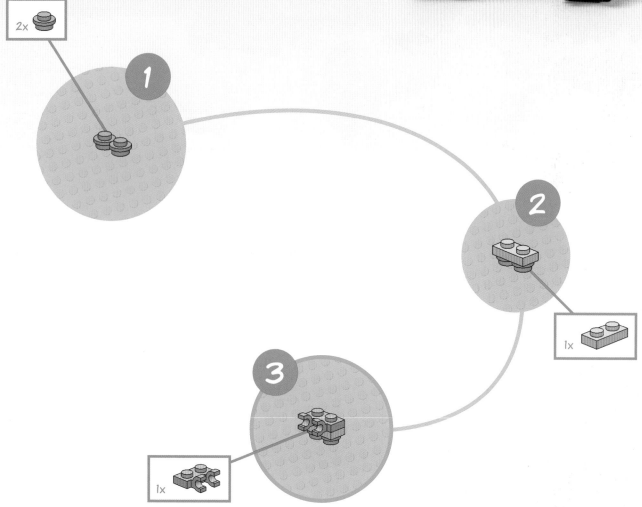

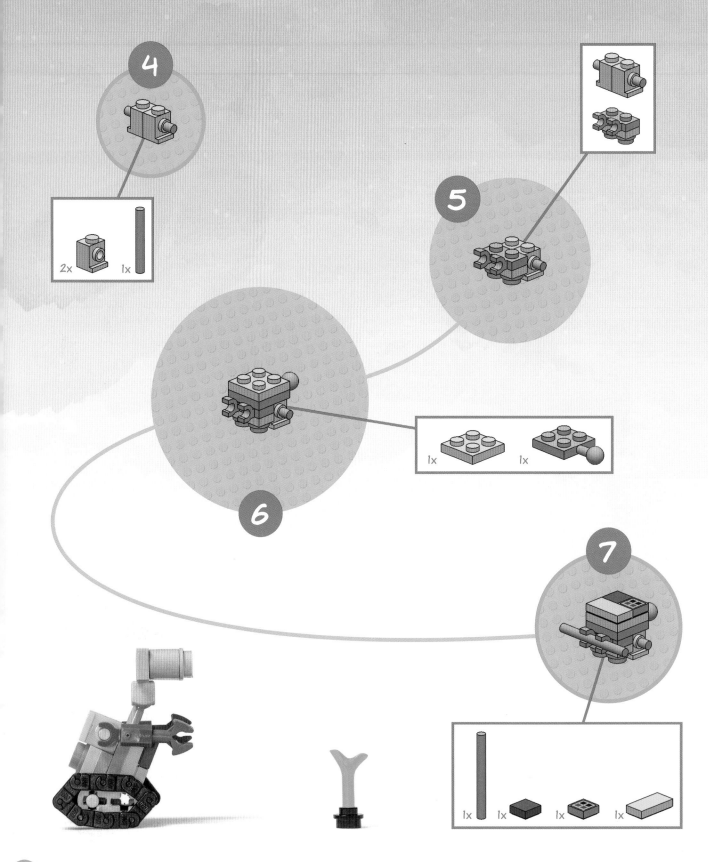

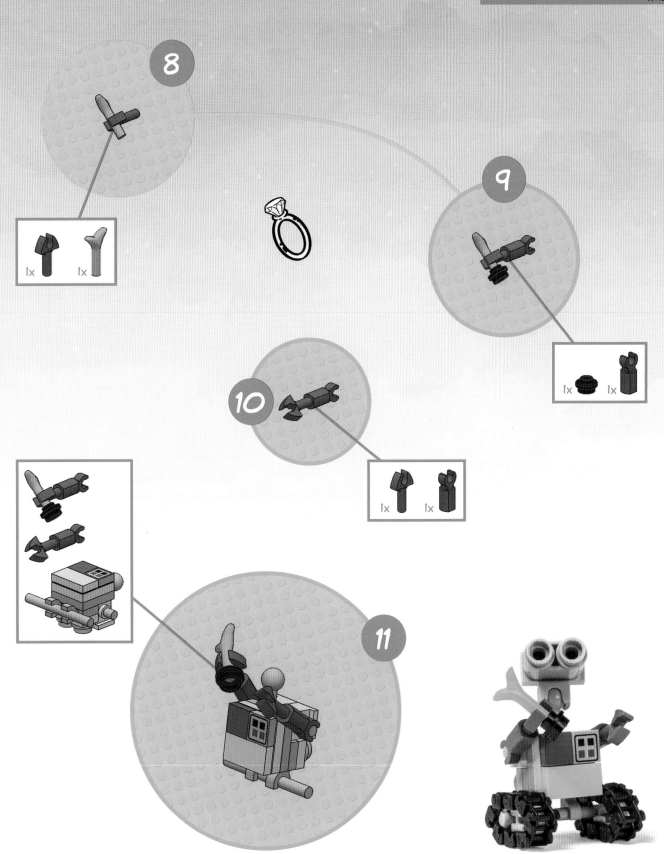

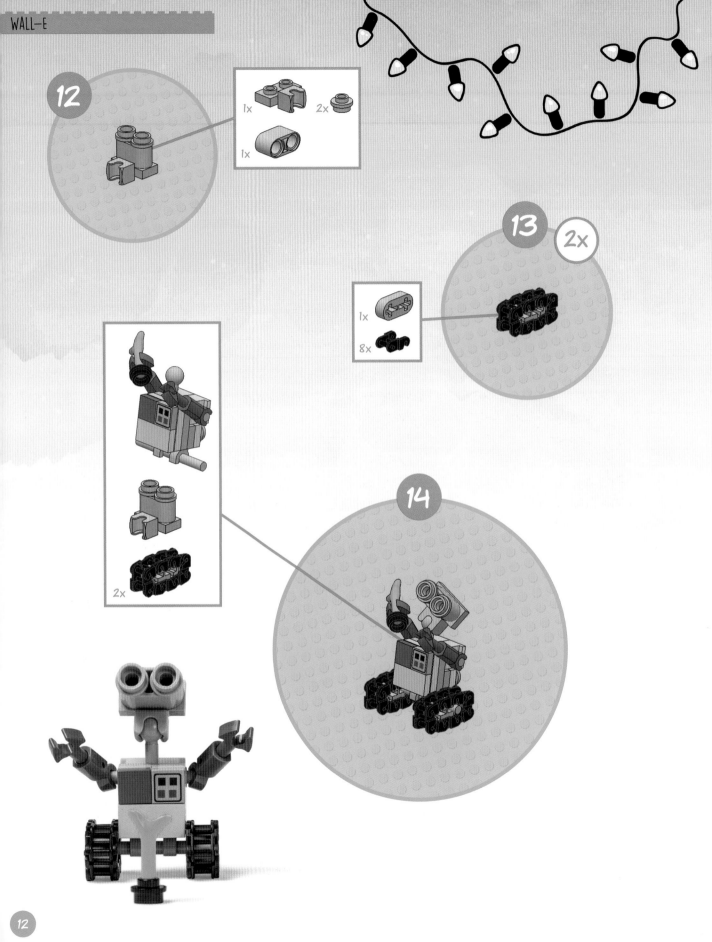

PARTS LIST

Quantity	Color		Element	Element Name	LEGO Number
2		Dark Bluish Gray	48729	Bar 1.5L with Clip	4222196, 4289542
1		Light Bluish Gray	30374	Bar 4L Light Sabre Blade	4211628, 6116608
1		Light Bluish Gray	87994	Bar 3L	6064033, 6093527
2		Dark Bluish Gray	11090	Bar Tube with Clip	6015890
2		Light Bluish Gray	43857	Technic Beam 2 x 1 Liftarm	4211862
2		Bright Light Orange	4070	Brick 1 x 1 with Headlight	6020098
1		Bright Green	33183	Minifig Food Carrot Top	4119479
2		Orange	4073	Plate 1 x 1 Round	4157103
1		Black	85861	Plate 1 x 1 Round with Open Stud	6100627
2		Light Bluish Gray	85861	Plate 1 x 1 Round with Open Stud	6124825
1		Bright Light Orange	3023	Plate 1 x 2	6028736
1		Light Bluish Gray	60470	Plate 1 x 2 with 2 Clips Horizontal	4515173, 4556157
1		Light Bluish Gray	14704	Plate 1 x 2 with Socket Joint-8 with Friction Centre	6043656
1		Bright Light Orange	3022	Plate 2 x 2	4243776, 6003033
1		Light Bluish Gray	3731	Plate 2 x 2 with Towball	4239654
2		Light Bluish Gray	41677	Technic Beam 2 x 0.5 Liftarm	4211741
16		Black	3711	Technic Chain Link	371126, 6044702
1		Dark Bluish Gray	3070b	Tile 1 x 1 with Groove	4210848
1		Light Bluish Gray	3070bp06	Tile 1 x 1 with Red & Black Buttons Pattern	
1		Bright Light Orange	3069b	Tile 1 x 2 with Groove	4622062

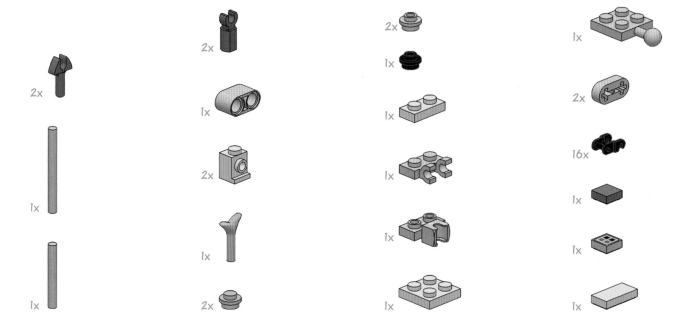

CLASSIC SPACE

The Classic Space series in the 1970s marked LEGO's first step into the boundless possibilities of science fiction. Even now, the design and color scheme of this space series still attract a loyal group of fans. Benny in The LEGO Movie is a perfect example of how Classic Space appeals to new as well as older fans.

In my quest to find models that can easily be created from as few pieces as possible, I turned my thoughts back to space sets from my own childhood and tried to recreate them in miniature. Have a go at experimenting with your own LEGO pieces: You could try using different colors or building a different model. Become a master builder—just like Benny in the movie!

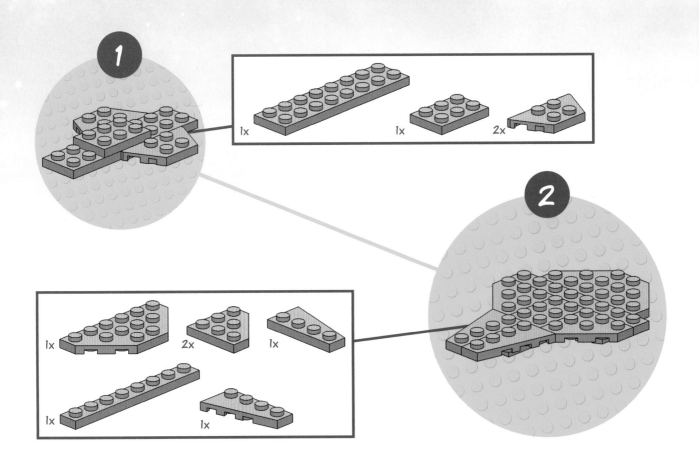

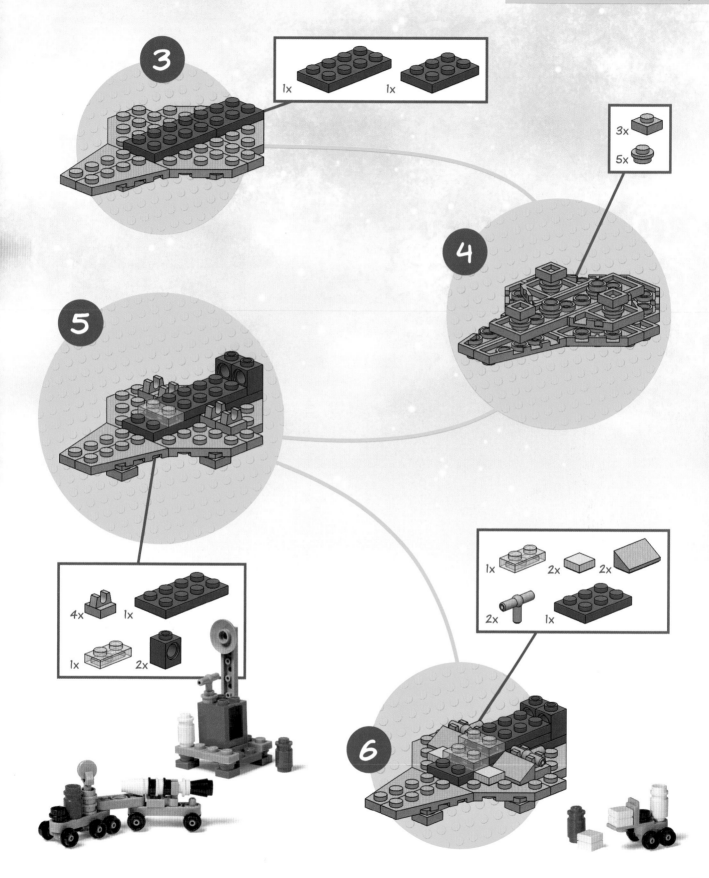

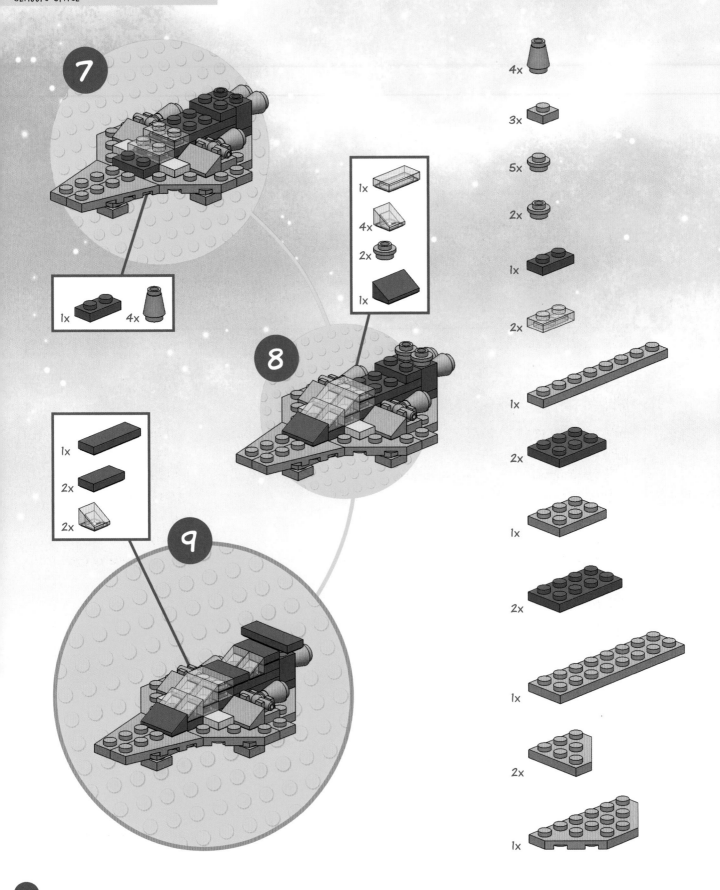

PARTS LIST

Quantity	Color		Element	Element Name	LEGO Number
4		Light Bluish Gray	4589b	Cone 1 x 1 with Stop	4211499, 4529241
3		Light Bluish Gray	3024	Plate 1 x 1	4211399
5		Light Bluish Gray	4073	Plate 1 x 1 Round	4211525
2		Light Bluish Gray	85861	Plate 1 x 1 Round with Open Stud	6124825
1		Blue	3023	Plate 1 x 2	302323
2		Trans Yellow	3023	Plate 1 x 2	4194746
1		Light Bluish Gray	3460	Plate 1 x 8	4211425
2		Blue	3021	Plate 2 x 3	302123
1		Light Bluish Gray	3021	Plate 2 x 3	4211396
2		Blue	3020	Plate 2 x 4	302023
1		Light Bluish Gray	3034	Plate 2 x 8	4211406
2		Light Bluish Gray	2450	Plate 3 x 3 without Corner	4211361
1		Light Bluish Gray	2419	Plate 3 x 6 without Corners	4211352
6		Trans Yellow	54200	Slope Brick 31 1 x 1 x 2/3	4244367, 4260942
1		Blue	85984	Slope Brick 31 1 x 2 x 0.667	4651236
2		Light Bluish Gray	85984	Slope Brick 31 1 x 2 x 0.667	4568637
2		Blue	6541	Technic Brick 1 x 1 with Hole	4119014
2		Light Bluish Gray	4697b	Technic Pneumatic T-Piece - Type 2	4211508
4		Light Bluish Gray	2555	Tile 1 x 1 with Clip	2555194, 4211369, 6030711
2		Yellow	3070b	Tile 1 x 1 with Groove	307024
2		Blue	3069b	Tile 1 x 2 with Groove	306923
1		Trans Yellow	3069b	Tile 1 x 2 with Groove	3007044, 306944, 4194535
1		Blue	63864	Tile 1 x 3 with Groove	4587840
2		Light Bluish Gray	51739	Wing 2 x 4	4252368, 4507056
1		Light Bluish Gray	41770	Wing 2 x 4 Left	4211735
1		Light Bluish Gray	41769	Wing 2 x 4 Right	4211732

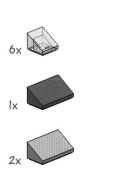

6x

1x

2x

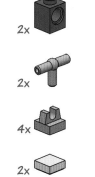

2x

2x

4x

2x

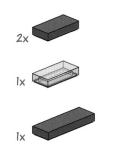

2x

1x

1x

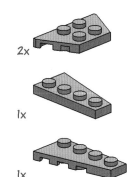

2x

1x

1x

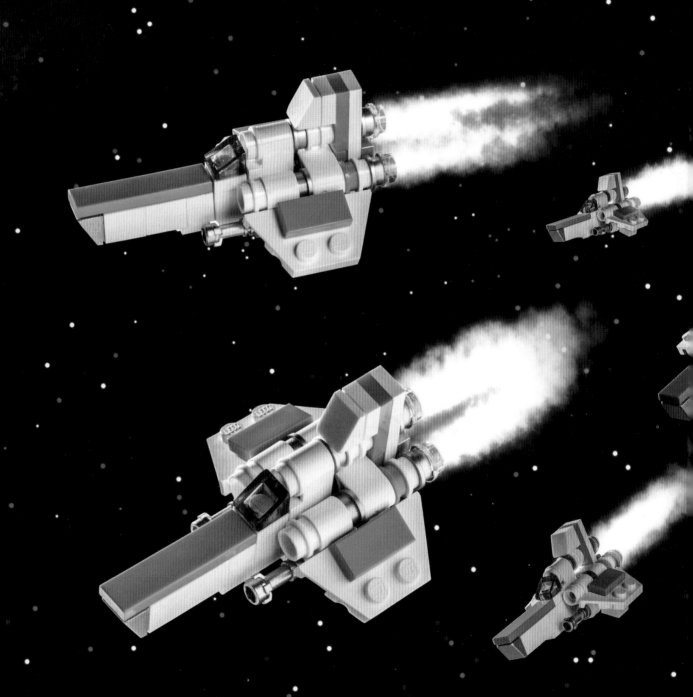

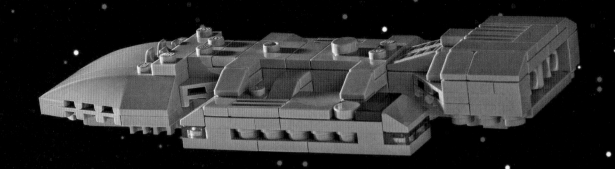

VIPER

Battlestar Galactica is a TV series I remember from childhood, which is currently enjoying a fresh wave of popularity among fans. A revised version of the series was produced quite recently and it is the Viper, in particular, which has evolved over the years to become a cult spacecraft. The model was originally designed in the 1970s by John Dykstra, who also developed the famous X-Wing Fighter for Star Wars. It is very simple to reproduce the different versions of the maneuverable Colonial Viper in LEGO simply by using different colors for the model.

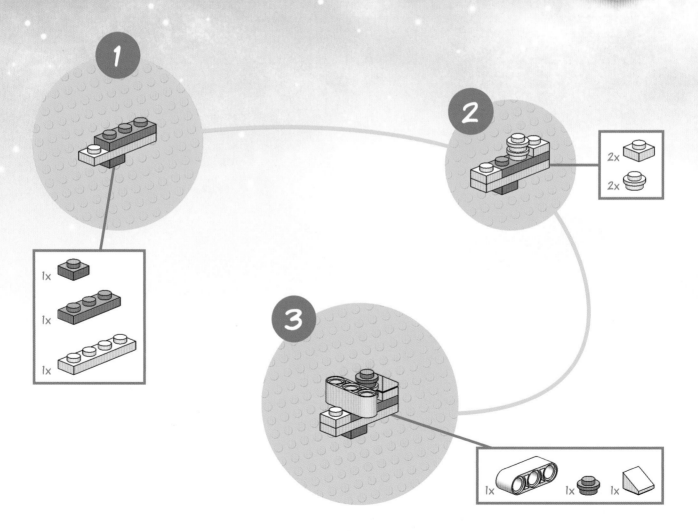

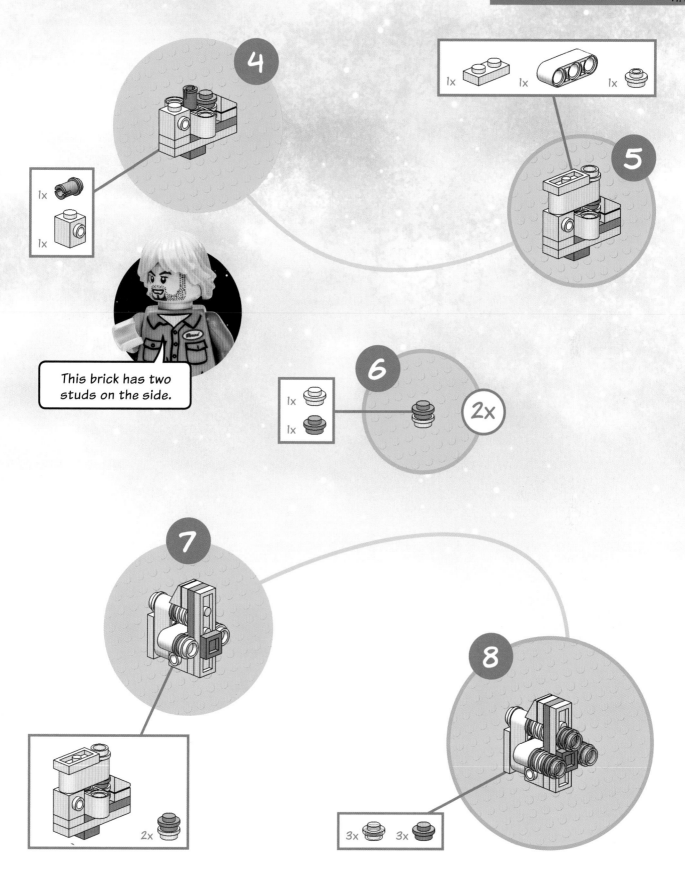

This brick has two studs on the side.

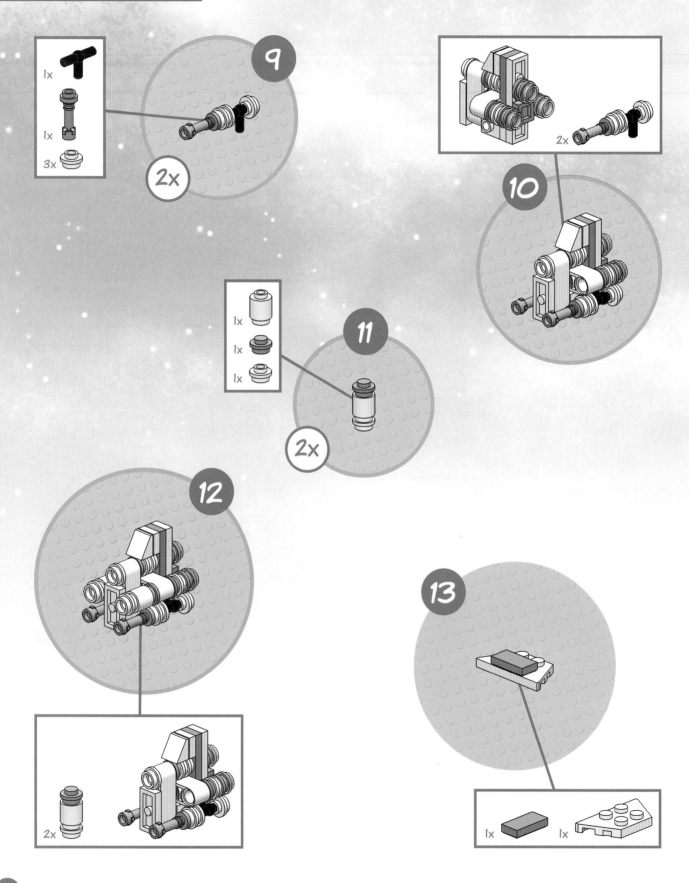

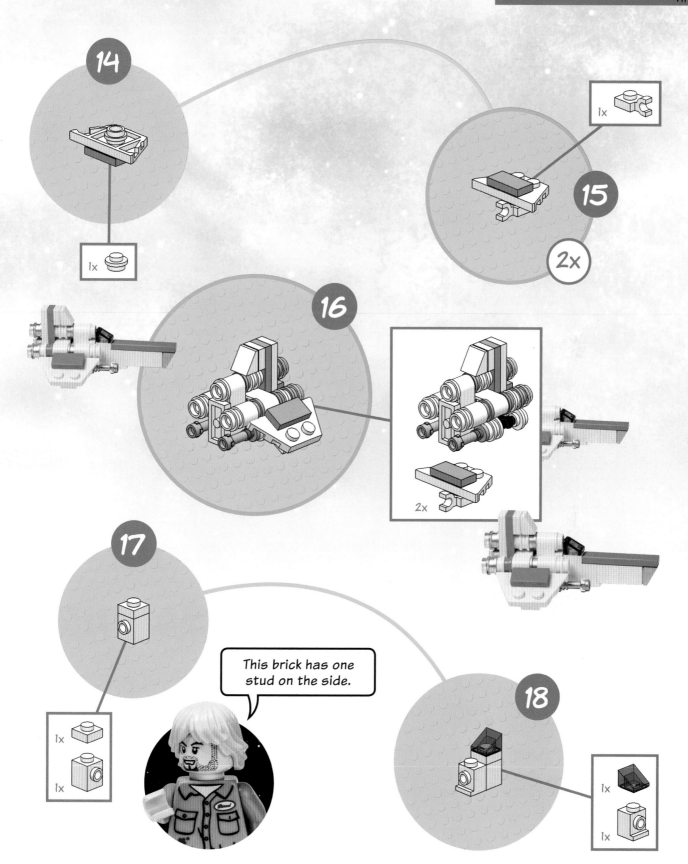

This brick has one stud on the side.

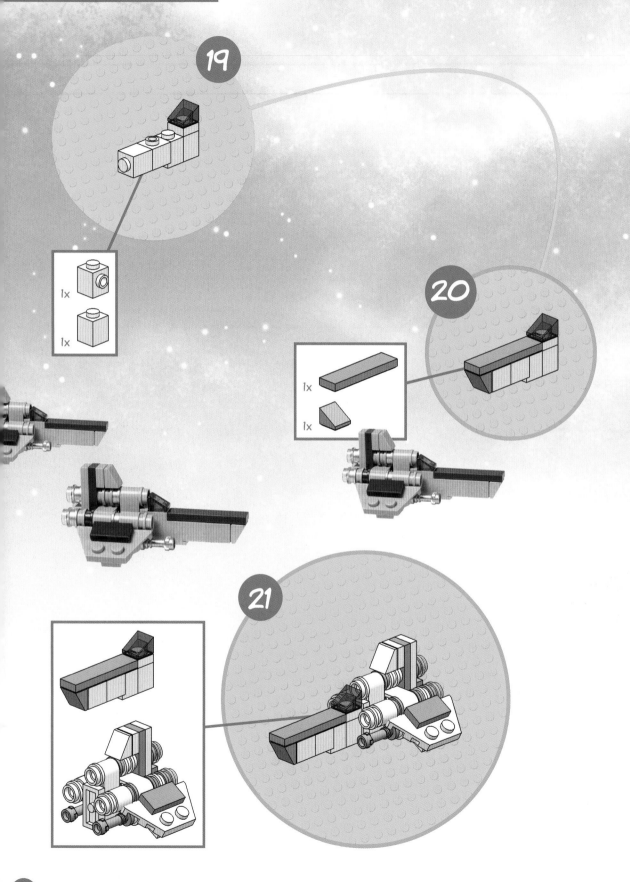

19

1x
1x

20

1x
1x

21

PARTS LIST

Quantity	Color	Element	Element Name	LEGO Number
1	White	3005	Brick 1 x 1	300501
2	White	3062b	Brick 1 x 1 Round with Hollow Stud	306201
1	White	4070	Brick 1 x 1 with Headlight	407001
1	White	87087	Brick 1 x 1 with Stud on 1 Side	4558952
2	White	47905	Brick 1 x 1 with Studs on Two Opposite Sides	4626882
2	Metallic Silver	64567	Minifig Tool Light Sabre Hilt	4542406, 4548731, 6051389
1	Metallic Silver	3024	Plate 1 x 1	4528732
3	White	3024	Plate 1 x 1	302401
6	Metallic_Silver	4073	Plate 1 x 1 Round	4249039, 51809301, 6051507
2	Orange	4073	Plate 1 x 1 Round	4157103
3	Trans Light Blue	4073	Plate 1 x 1 Round	unbekannt
6	White	4073	Plate 1 x 1 Round	614101
9	White	85861	Plate 1 x 1 Round with Open Stud	4547649
2	White	6019	Plate 1 x 1 with Clip Horizontal	601901
1	White	3023	Plate 1 x 2	302301
1	Orange	3623	Plate 1 x 3	4219920, 4513281
1	White	3710	Plate 1 x 4	371001
1	Metallic Silver	54200	Slope Brick 31 1 x 1 x 2/3	4528609, 6092109
1	Trans Black	54200	Slope Brick 31 1 x 1 x 2/3	4244368
1	White	54200	Slope Brick 31 1 x 1 x 2/3	4244370, 4504369
2	White	32523	Technic Beam 3	4157772, 4208160
1	Light Bluish Gray	4274	Technic Pin 1/2	4211483, 4274194
2	Black	4697b	Technic Pneumatic T-Piece - Type 2	6104209
2	Orange	3069b	Tile 1 x 2 with Groove	4188771
1	Orange	2431	Tile 1 x 4 with Groove	4160593
2	White	51739	Wing 2 x 4	4249506

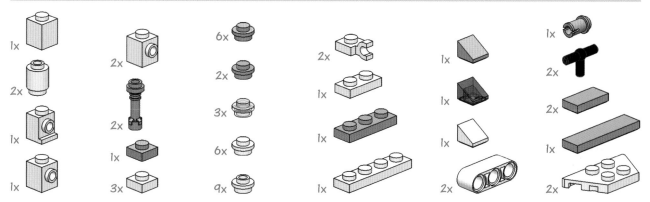

STARSHIP ENTERPRISE

A constant succession of new
TV series and movies has kept the Star Trek
cult alive for generations! I, for one, built the original
version of the spacecraft as well as a corresponding
Warbird, although it is unlikely that most people's collections will include the large 8x8 tile and the nozzle
that I used for the neck. Nevertheless, I still maintain that these are the perfect pieces for creating a scale
model of the Enterprise that is as close to the original as possible. But perhaps you master builders out
there will come up with even more ideas of your own and surprise me with your suggestions.

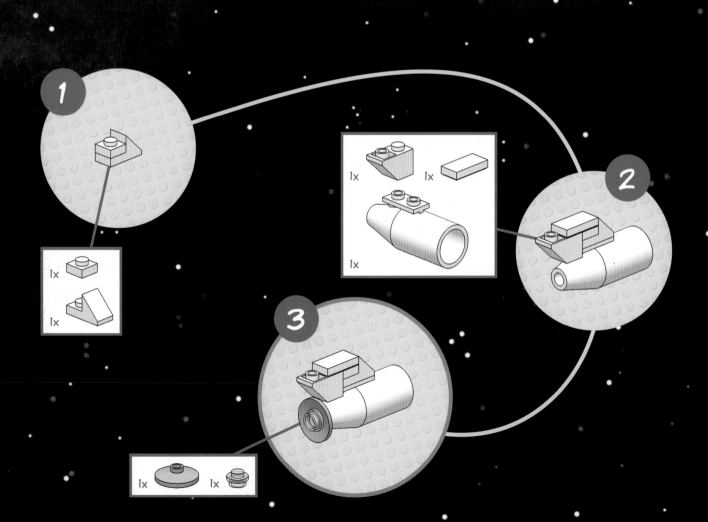

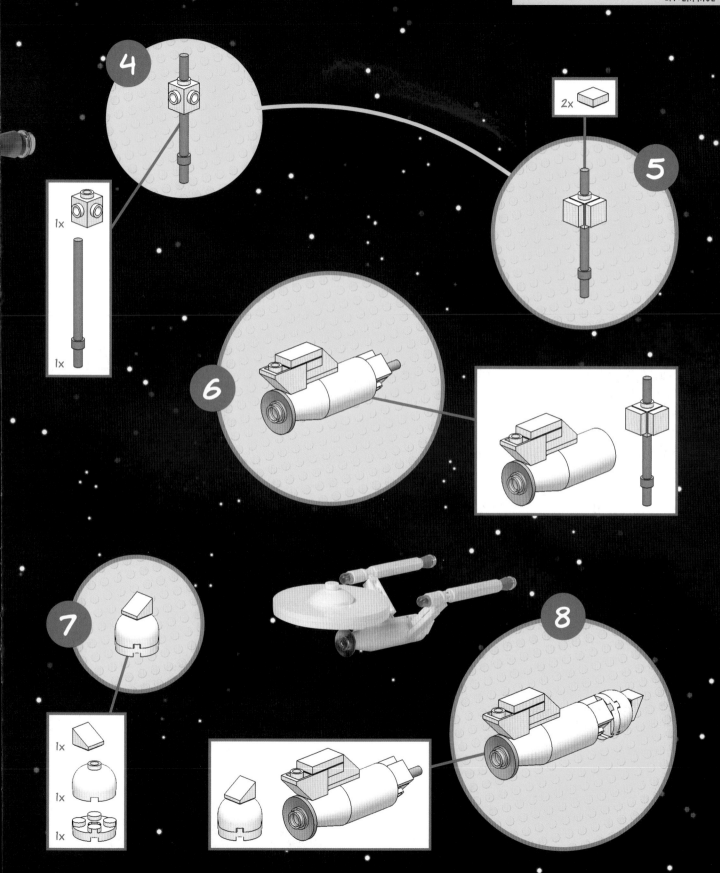

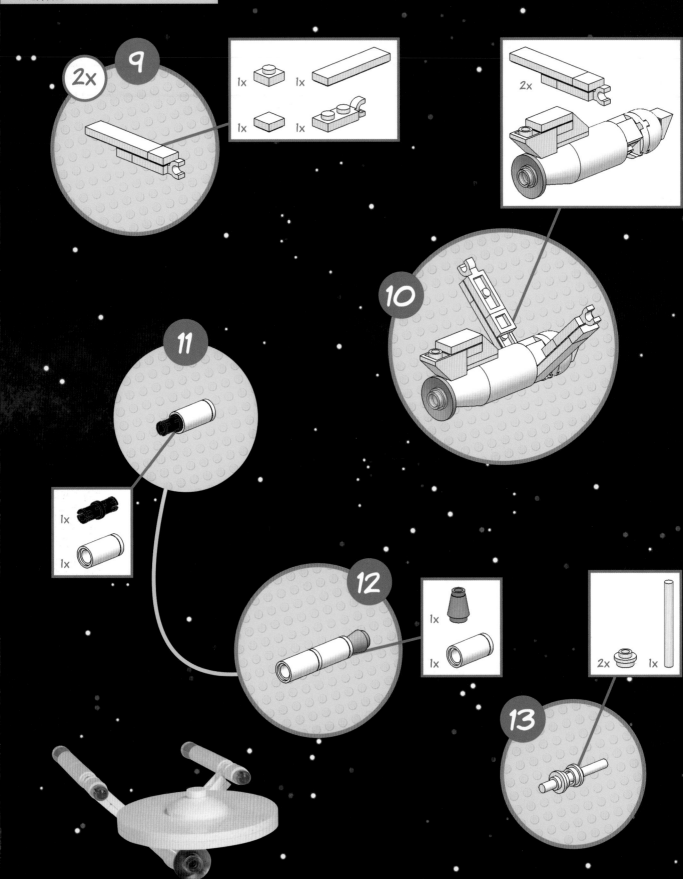

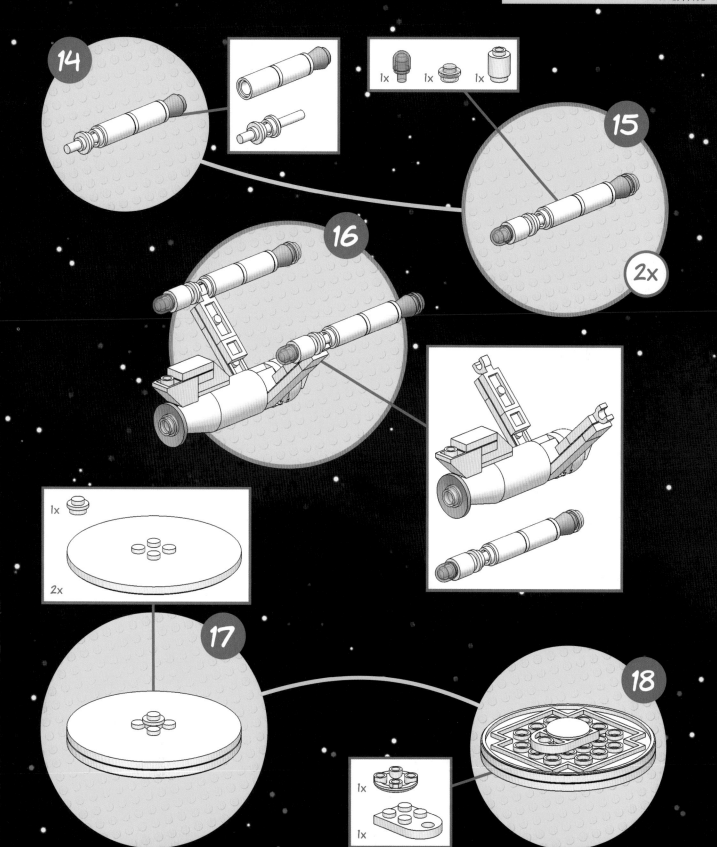

19

1x

1x

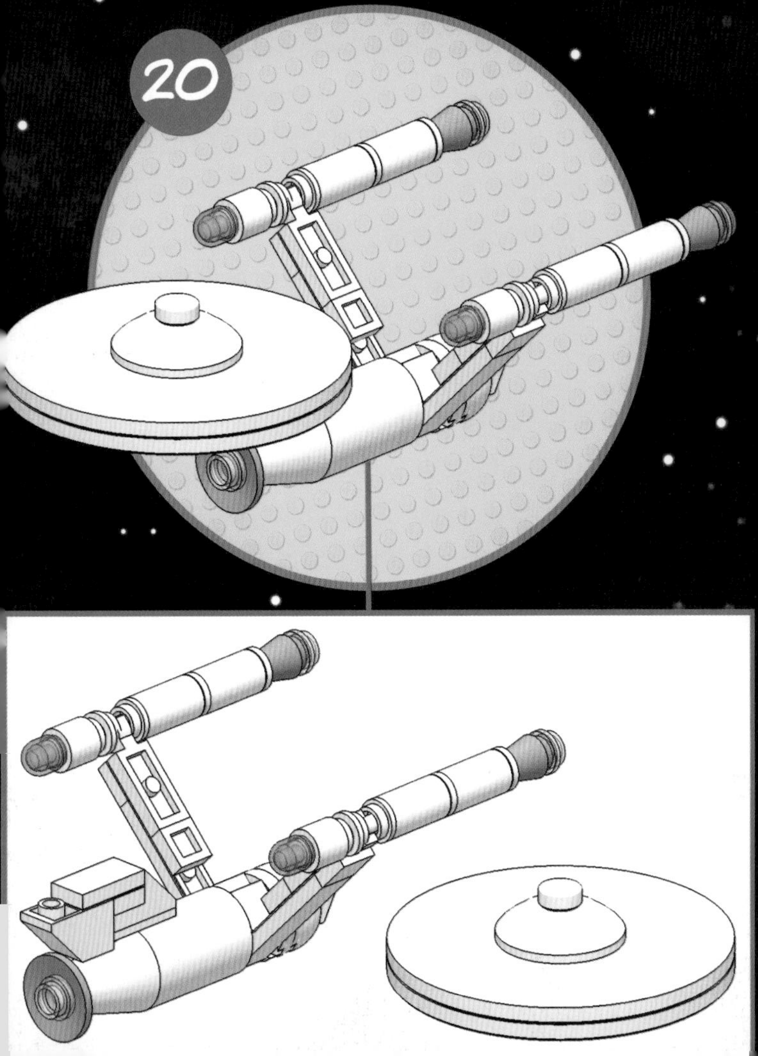

20

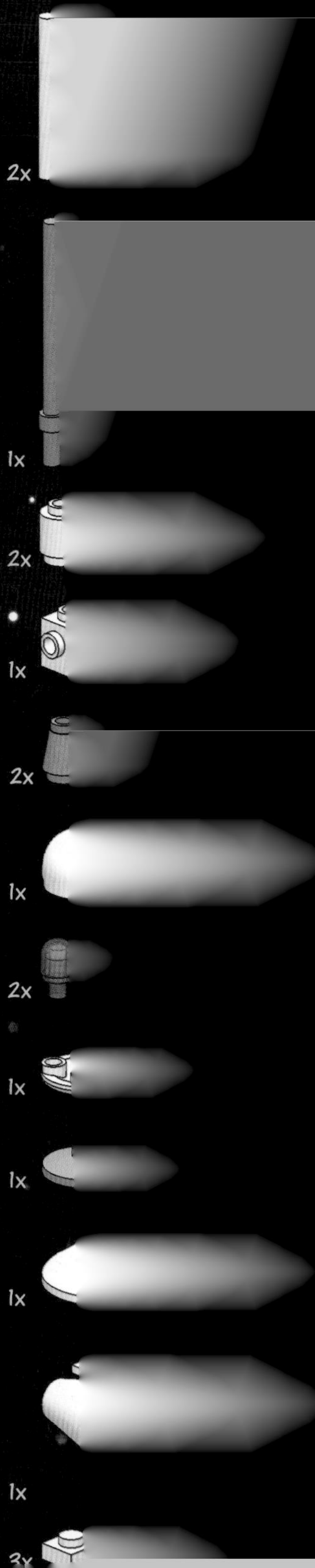

2x

1x

2x

1x

2x

1x

2x

1x

1x

1x

1x

3x

PARTS LIST

Quantity	Color	Element	Element Name	LEGO Number
2	White	30374	Bar 4L Light Sabre Blade	4129836, 6116602
1	Light Bluish Gray	63965	Bar 6L with Thick Stop	4538098, 6061535, 6081975
2	White	3062b	Brick 1 x 1 Round with Hollow Stud	306201
1	White	4733	Brick 1 x 1 with Studs on Four Sides	4111971
2	Light Bluish Gray	4589b	Cone 1 x 1 with Stop	4211499, 4529241
1	White	30367	Cylinder 2 x 2 with Dome Top	4124120
2	Trans Orange	58176	Cylinder Domed 1 x 1 x 1.667 with Bar	4524365
1	White	2654	Dish 2 x 2	265401, 4278271
1	Metallic Gold	4740	Dish 2 x 2 Inverted	6078236
1	White	43898	Dish 3 x 3 Inverted	4179580
1	White	4868a	Plane Jet Engine	unbekannt
3	White	3024	Plate 1 x 1	302401
3	Trans Light Blue	4073	Plate 1 x 1 Round	4163917
1	White	4073	Plate 1 x 1 Round	614101
4	White	85861	Plate 1 x 1 Round with Open Stud	4547649
2	White	63868	Plate 1 x 2 with Clip Horizontal on End	4535737
1	White	4032b	Plate 2 x 2 Round with Axlehole Type 2	403201
1	White	3176	Plate 3 x 2 with Hole	4241007, 6089696
1	White	54200	Slope Brick 31 1 x 1 x 2/3	4244370, 4504369
1	White	3665	Slope Brick 45 2 x 1 Inverted	366501
1	White	92946	Slope Plate 45 2 x 1	6015912, 6069002
4	White	75535	Technic Pin Joiner Round	75535
2	Black	2780	Technic Pin with Friction	278026, 4121715
1	White	98138	Tile 1 x 1 Round with Groove	4646844
4	White	3070b	Tile 1 x 1 with Groove	307001
1	White	3069b	Tile 1 x 2 with Groove	306901
2	White	2431	Tile 1 x 4 with Groove	243101
2	White	6177	Tile 8 x 8 Round with 2 x 2 Center Studs	

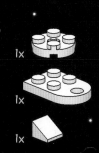

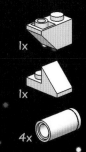

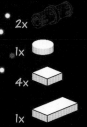

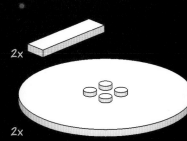

WARBIRD

This is a Klingon Warbird. Bird of Prey was the name initially given to the spacecraft that followed on from these spaceships. The Cruiser would obviously look better in dark green but LEGO pieces are rarely available in this color, which is why, when compiling the assembly instructions, I opted for a shade of green that is more likely to be found in everyone's LEGO box.

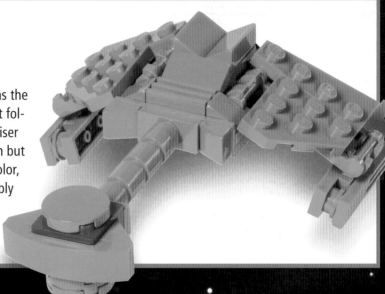

1

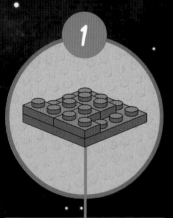

2x

1x

1x

2

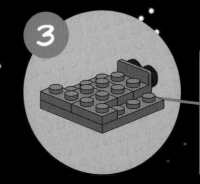

2x   1x

3

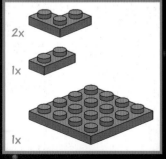

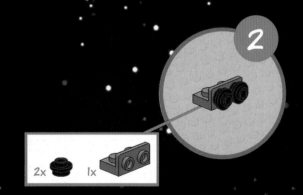

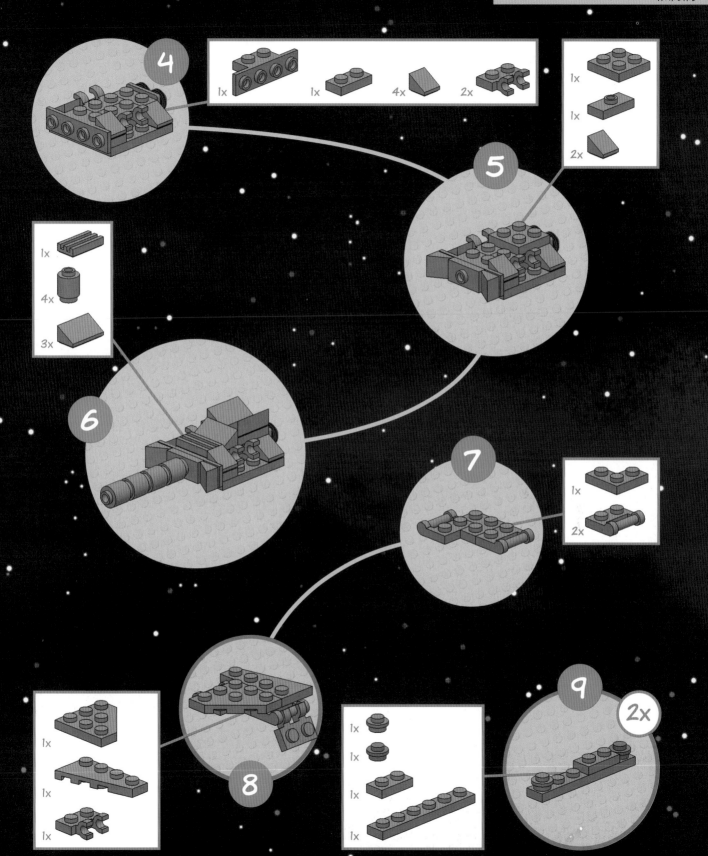

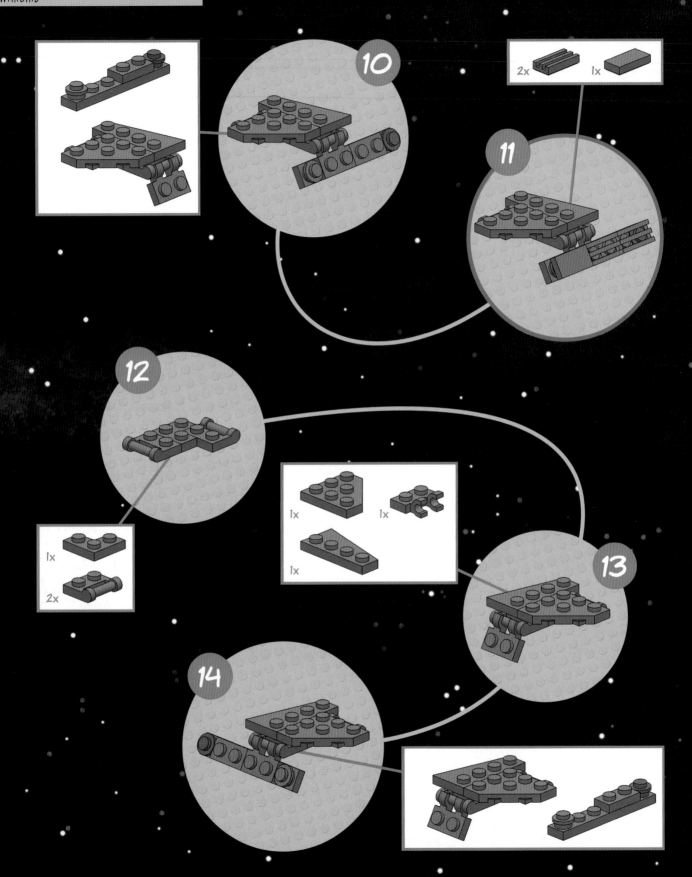

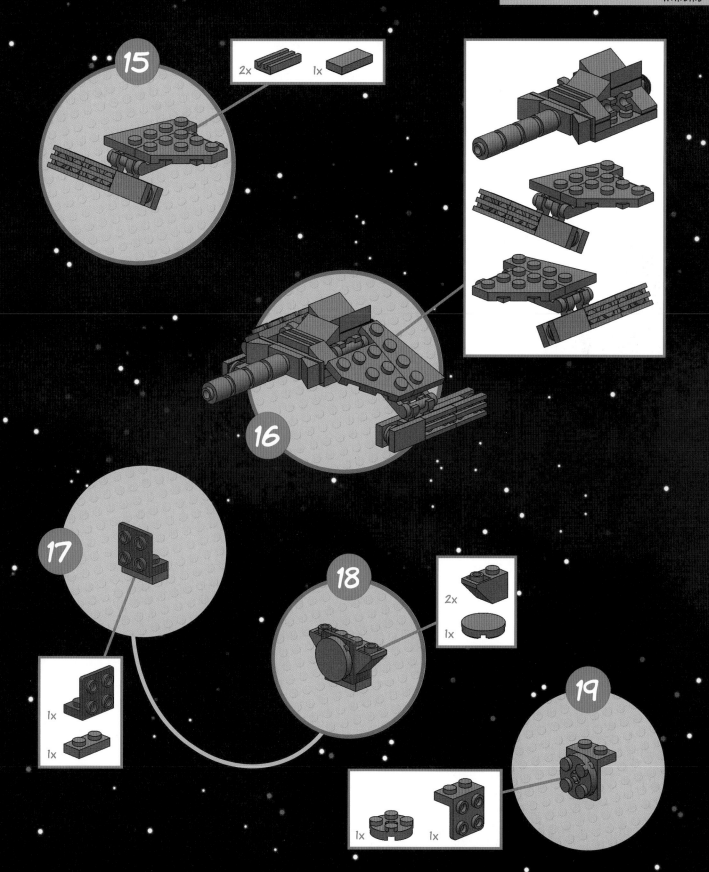

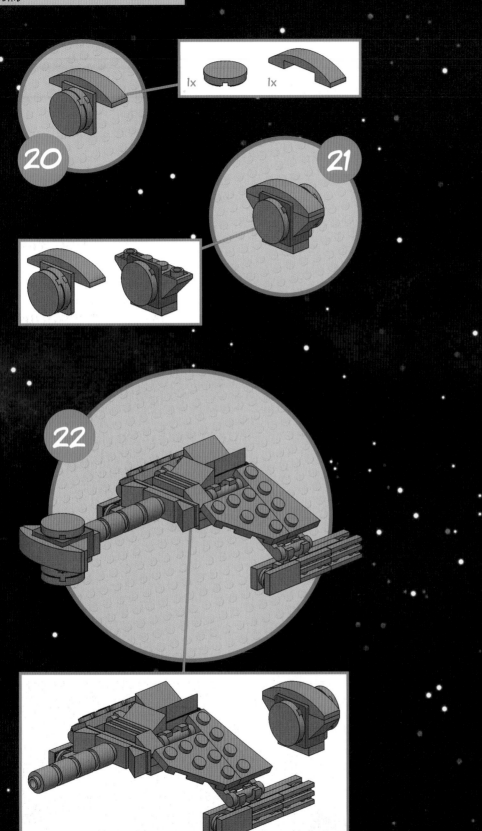

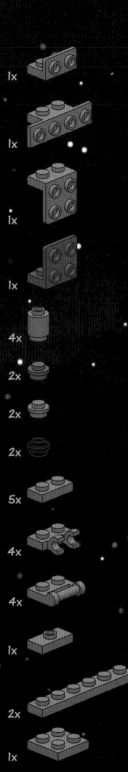

1x

1x

1x

1x

4x

2x

2x

2x

5x

4x

4x

1x

2x

1x

4x

1x

PARTS LIST

Quantity	Color		Element	Element Name	LEGO Number
1		Green	99780	Bracket 1 x 2 - 1 x 2 Up	6099243
1		Green	2436a	Bracket 1 x 2 - 1 x 4 Type 1	4280152, 4282747
1		Green	44728	Bracket 1 x 2 - 2 x 2	4212471, 6048853, 6117971
1		Red	99207	Bracket 1 x 2 - 2 x 2 Up	6001806
4		Green	3062b	Brick 1 x 1 Round with Hollow Stud	306228
2		Dark Bluish Gray	4073	Plate 1 x 1 Round	4210633
2		Green	4073	Plate 1 x 1 Round	4218588, 4519965, 4569058
2		Black	85861	Plate 1 x 1 Round with Open Stud	6100627
5		Green	3023	Plate 1 x 2	302328
4		Green	60470	Plate 1 x 2 with 2 Clips Horizontal	4520671, 4556159
4		Green	48336	Plate 1 x 2 with Handle Type 2	4521931
1		Green	3794a	Plate 1 x 2 without Groove with 1 Centre Stud	379428
2		Green	3666	Plate 1 x 6	366628
1		Green	3022	Plate 2 x 2	302228
4		Green	2420	Plate 2 x 2 Corner	4157120
1		Green	4032b	Plate 2 x 2 Round with Axlehole Type 2	403228
3		Green	2450	Plate 3 x 3 without Corner	4240408, 6114672
1		Green	3031	Plate 4 x 4	4113158, 4243821
6		Green	54200	Slope Brick 31 1 x 1 x 2/3	4546705
3		Green	85984	Slope Brick 31 1 x 2 x 0.667	6000071
2		Green	3665	Slope Brick 45 2 x 1 Inverted	4142989
1		Green	93273	Slope Brick Curved 4 x 1 Double	6021539
5		Green	2412b	Tile 1 x 2 Grille with Groove	4141999, 4519978, 4568993
2		Green	3069b	Tile 1 x 2 with Groove	306928
2		Green	4150	Tile 2 x 2 Round with Cross Underside Stud	4239006
1		Green	41770	Wing 2 x 4 Left	4161334, 4543262
1		Green	41769	Wing 2 x 4 Right	4160871, 4543259

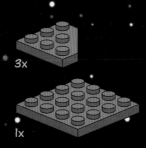

3x

1x

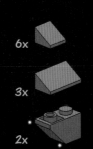

6x

3x

2x

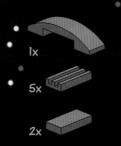

1x

5x

2x

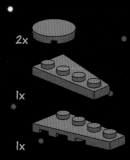

2x

1x

1x

SHUTTLE

This Star Trek Shuttle Columbus was attached to the USS Enterprise NCC-1701 during the days of Captain James T. Kirk. This F Class Shuttle is easy to reproduce as a microscale model.

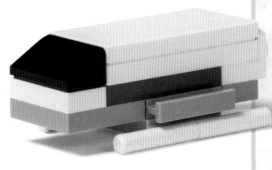

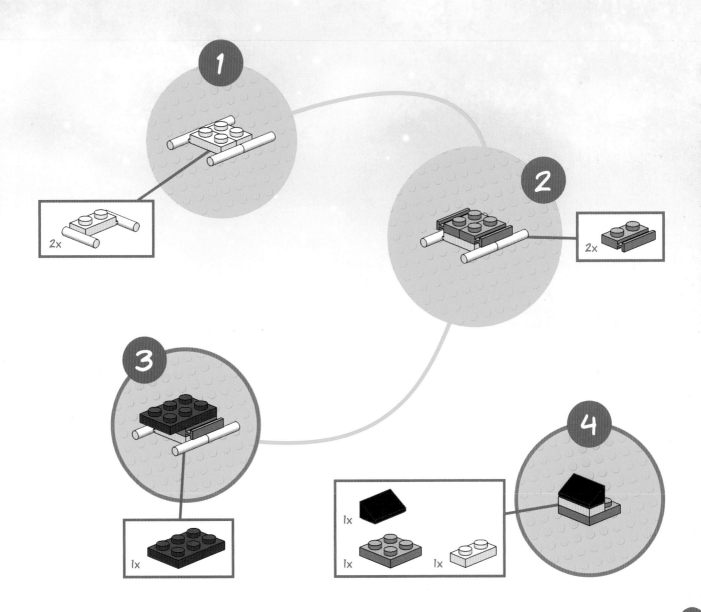

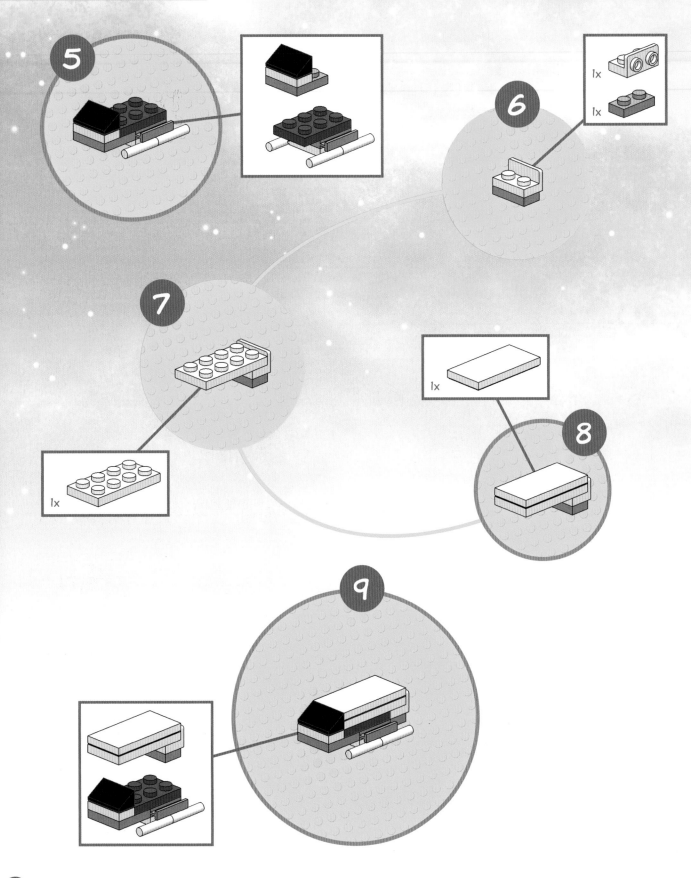

PARTS LIST

Quantity	Color		Element	Element Name	LEGO Number
2		Light Bluish Gray	32028	Plate 1 x 2 with Door Rail	4211568
1		White	99780	Bracket 1 x 2 - 1 x 2 Up	6070698
1		Light Bluish Gray	3023	Plate 1 x 2	3023194, 4211398
1		White	3023	Plate 1 x 2	302301
2		White	3839b	Plate 1 x 2 with Handles Type 2	383901
1		Light Bluish Gray	3022	Plate 2 x 2	4211397
1		Red	3021	Plate 2 x 3	302121
1		White	3020	Plate 2 x 4	302001
1		Black	85984	Slope Brick 31 1 x 2 x 0.667	4548180
1		White	87079	Tile 2 x 4 with Groove	4560178

2x

1x

1x

1x

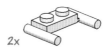
2x

1x

1x

1x

1x

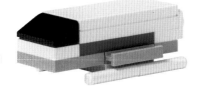

BLASTER

The Blaster is the most commonly used energy weapon in the Star Wars galaxy, ranging considerably in size and power.
I chose to build a larger version, which goes brilliantly with my Han Solo figure—reflecting his comment: "Hokey religions and ancient weapons are no match for a good blaster at your side."

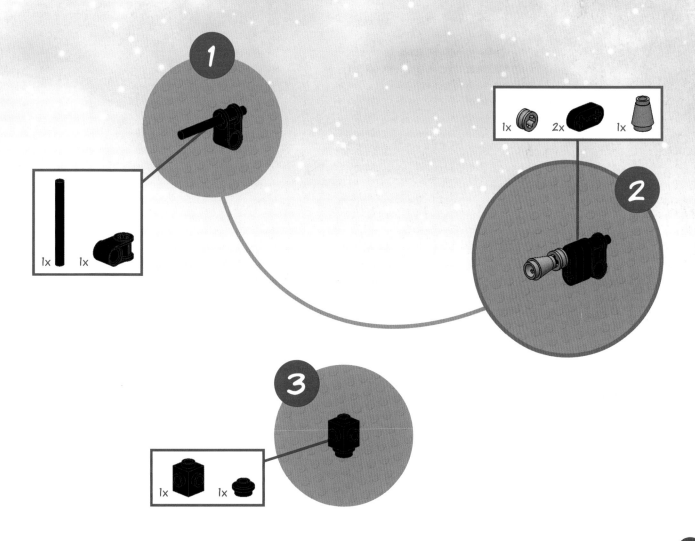

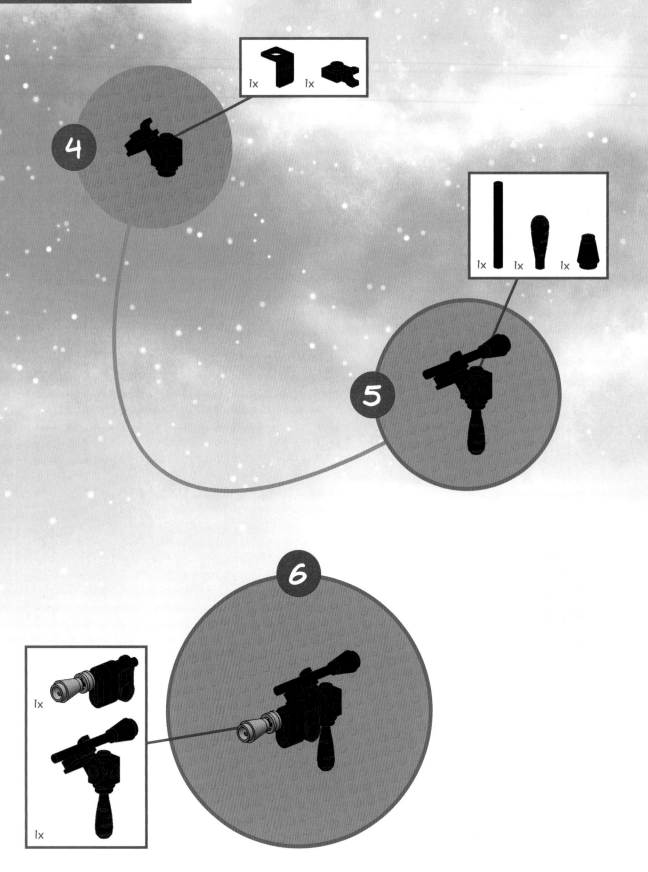

PARTS LIST

Quantity	Color		Element	Element Name	LEGO Number
2		Black	30374	Bar 4L Light Sabre Blade	3037426, 4140303, 6116604
1		Black	42446	Bracket 1 x 1 - 1 x 1	4169047, 4261427, 6020192
1		Black	4733	Brick 1 x 1 with Studs on Four Sides	473326
1		Black	4589b	Cone 1 x 1 with Stop	4518219, 4529236, 458926
1		Light Bluish Gray	4589b	Cone 1 x 1 with Stop	4211499, 4529241
1		Dark_Brown	33172	Minifig Food Carrot	4521781
1		Black	85861	Plate 1 x 1 Round with Open Stud	6100627
1		Black	6019	Plate 1 x 1 with Clip Horizontal	601926
2		Black	41677	Technic Beam 2 x 0.5 Liftarm	4164133, 4167726
1		Light Bluish Gray	32123	Technic Bush 1/2 Smooth with Axle Hole Reduced	4211573
1		Black	6536	Technic Cross Block 1 x 2 (Axle/Pin)	4173668, 653626

HAN SOLO

A model of a solitary Blaster among so many spacecraft would have been very uninteresting so I devised the figure of Han Solo to go with it. What I wanted to do was create a movable version of the Block Head figures included in the book Build Your Own Galaxy. As you can see over the next few pages, he has become extremely posable. I call this new design of figure Block Head 2.0. If you are a fan of this type of figure, you will find it simple—using this type of building technique—to create lots of other figures. Go ahead, try it for yourself!

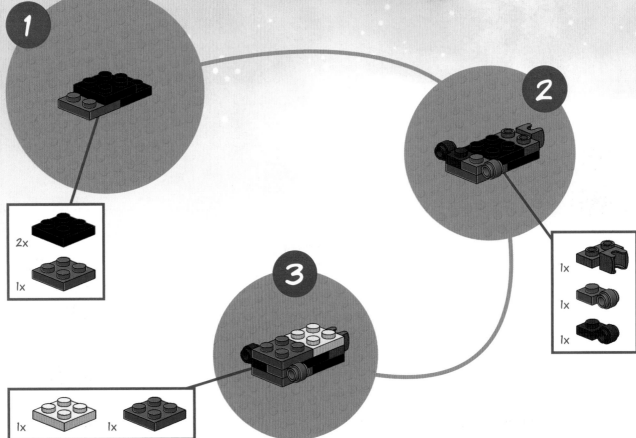

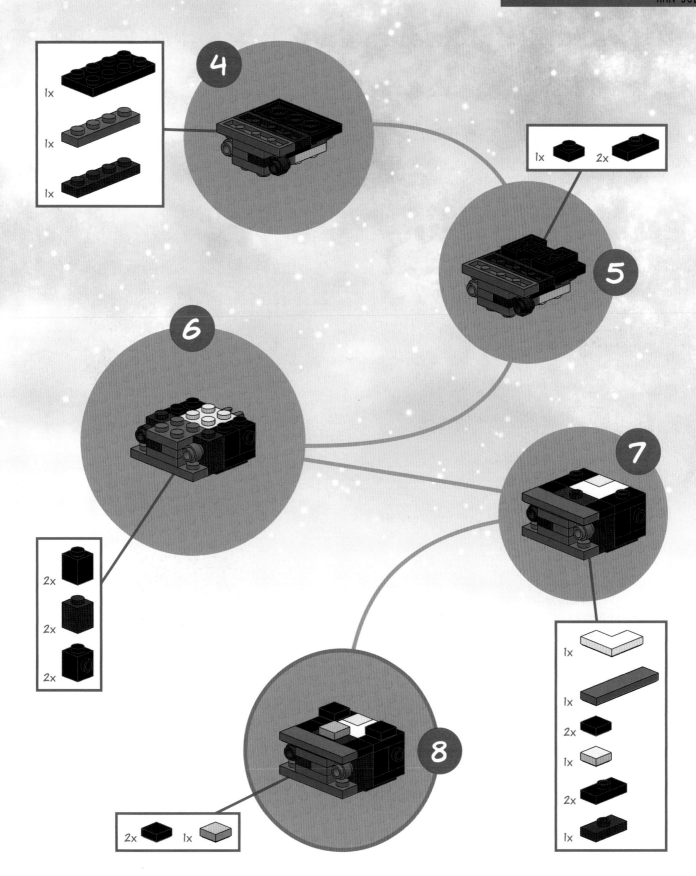

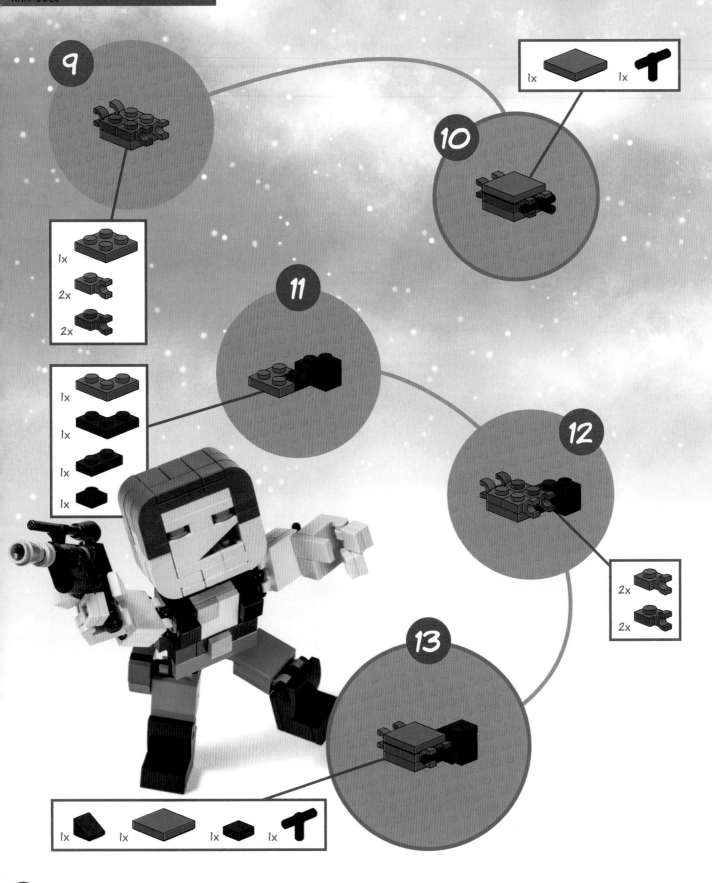

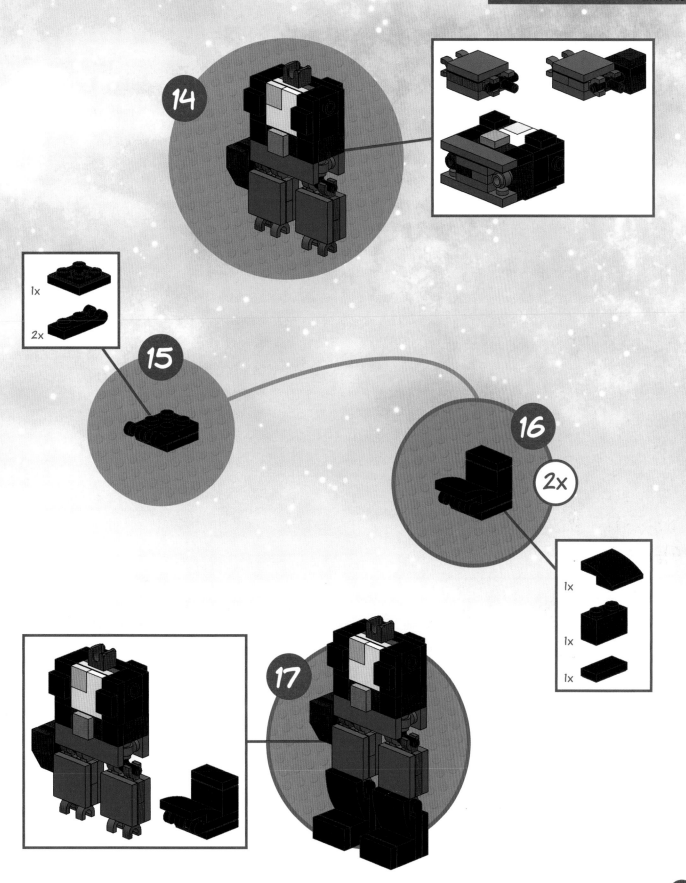

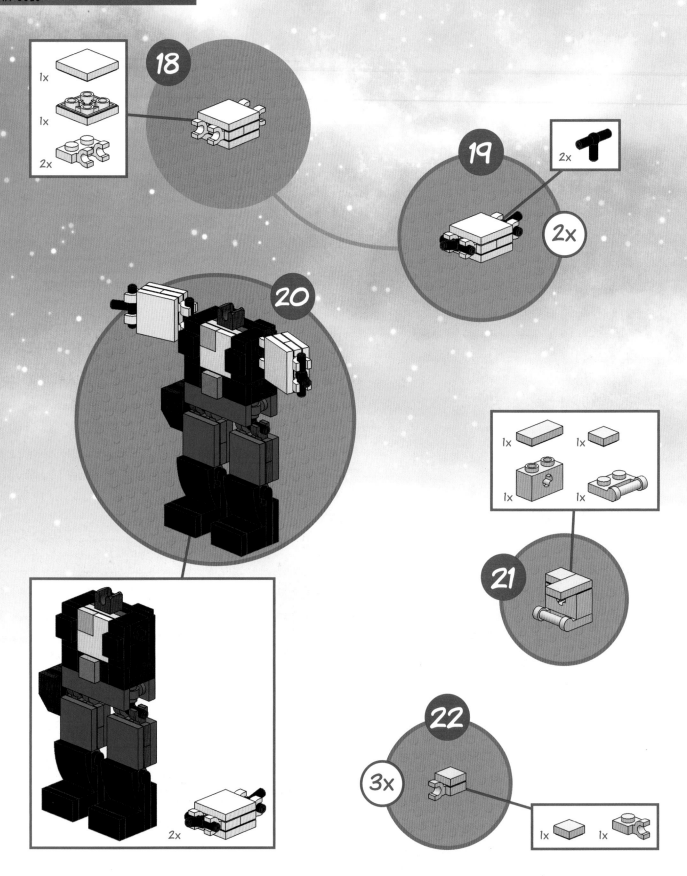

18

1x
1x
2x

19
2x
2x

20

21
1x 1x
1x 1x

2x

22
3x
1x 1x

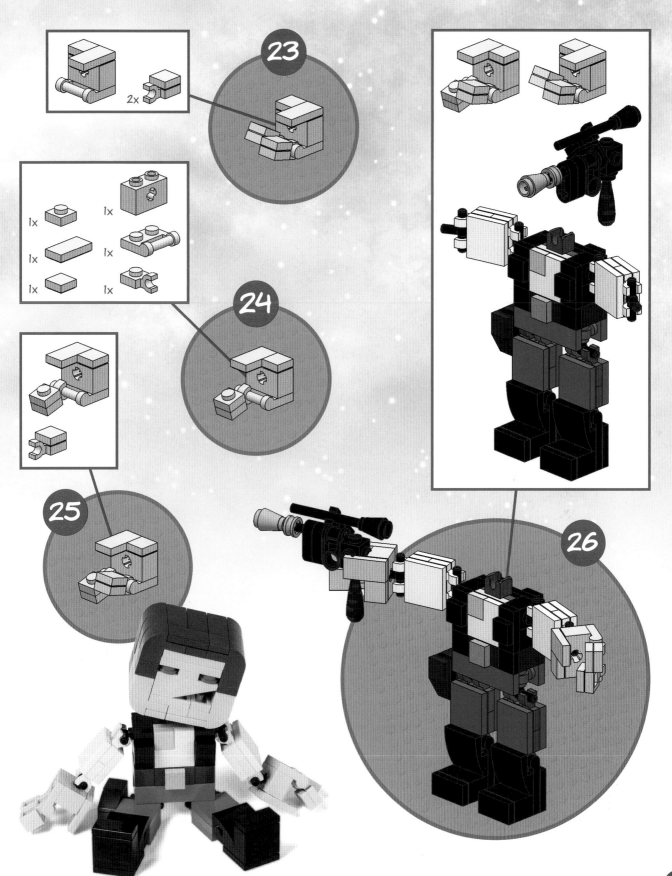

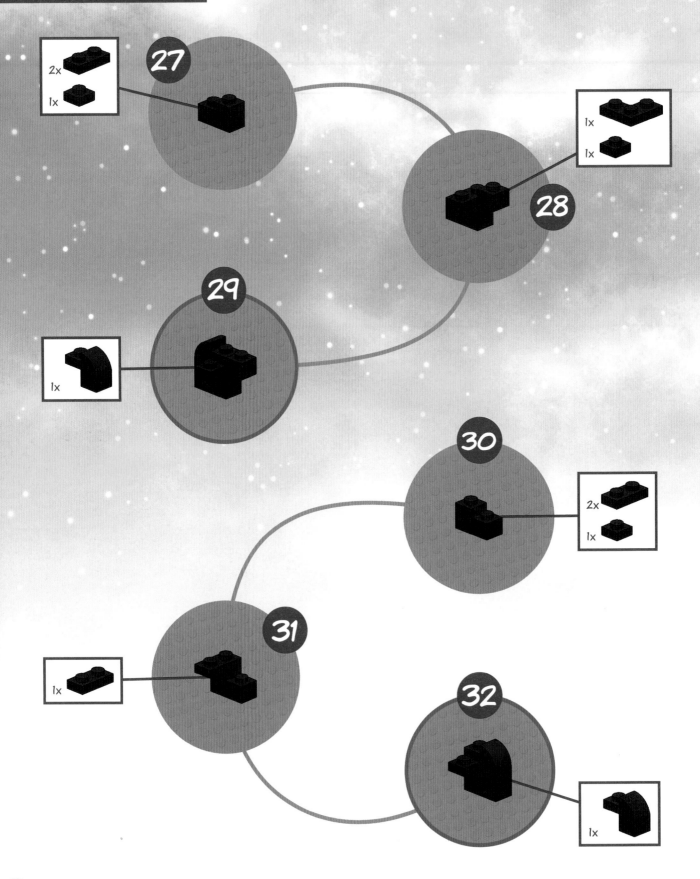

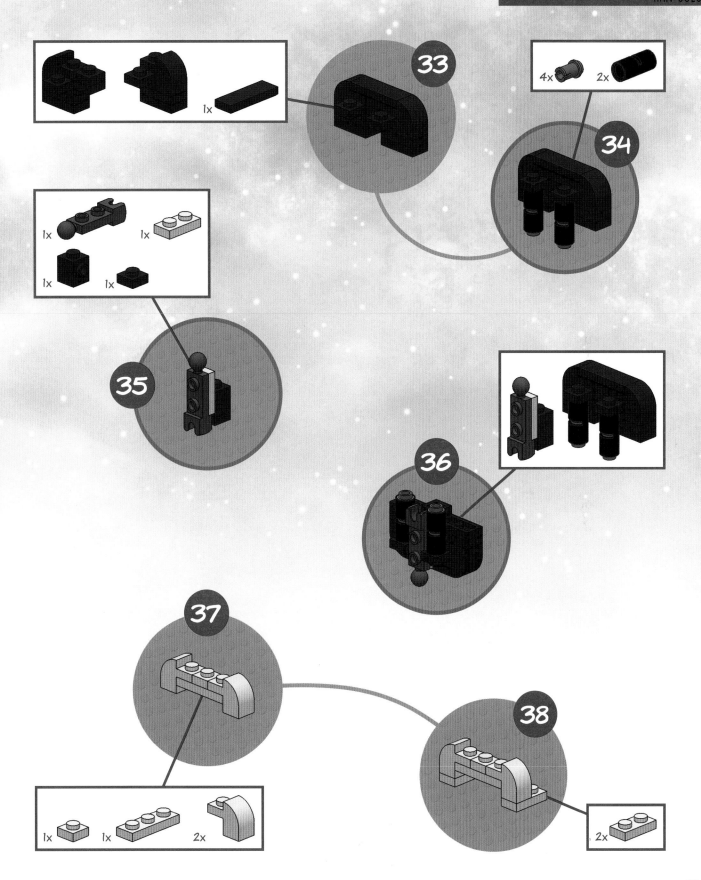

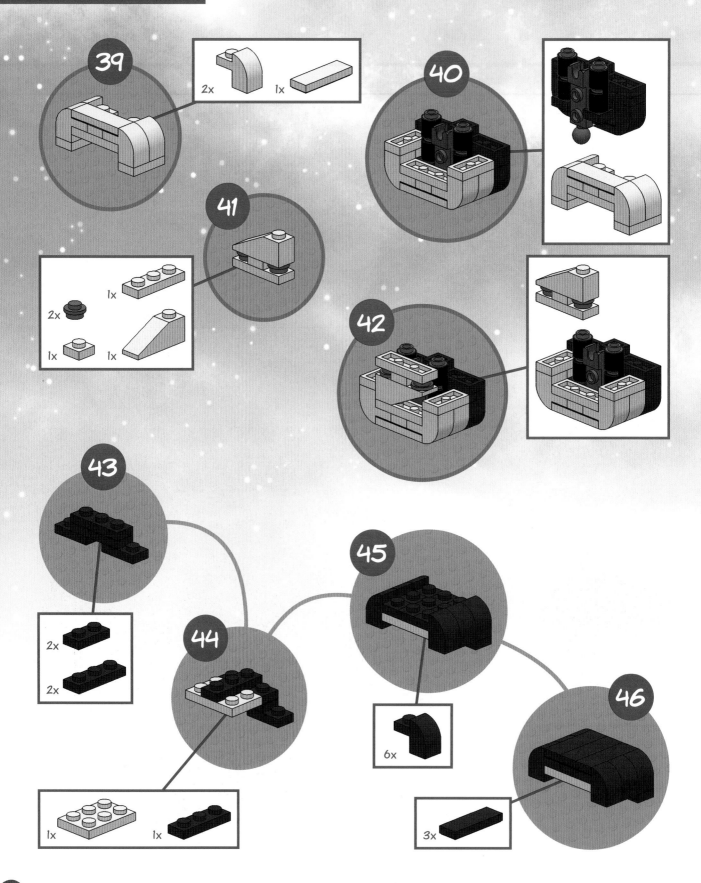

47

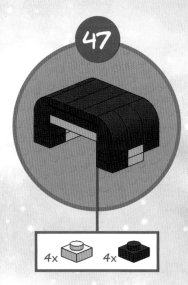

4x  4x

48

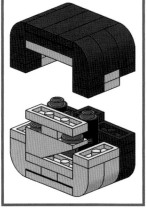

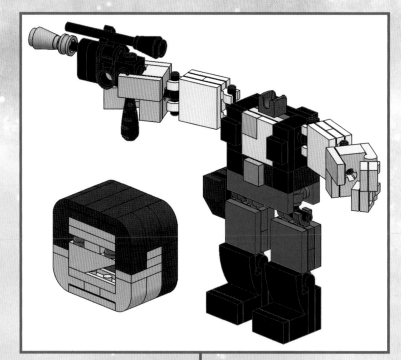

49

PARTS LIST

Quantity	Color	Element	Element Name	LEGO Number
2	Black	3005	Brick 1 x 1	300526
2	Reddish Brown	3005	Brick 1 x 1	4211242
2	Black	87087	Brick 1 x 1 with Stud on 1 Side	4558954
1	Reddish Brown	87087	Brick 1 x 1 with Stud on 1 Side	4618545, 6062574
2	Black	3004	Brick 1 x 2	300426
8	Reddish Brown	6091	Brick 2 x 1 x 1 & 1/3 with Curved Top	4505458, 4541261, 6035547
4	Tan	6091	Brick 2 x 1 x 1 & 1/3 with Curved Top	4125227, 4273526
2	Black	3024	Plate 1 x 1	302426
8	Reddish Brown	3024	Plate 1 x 1	4221744
7	Tan	3024	Plate 1 x 1	4159553
2	Blue	4073	Plate 1 x 1 Round	614123
4	Blue	6019	Plate 1 x 1 with Clip Horizontal	601923
4	Red	6019	Plate 1 x 1 with Clip Horizontal	601921
4	Tan	6019	Plate 1 x 1 with Clip Horizontal	4222034
1	Blue	4081b	Plate 1 x 1 with Clip Light Type 2	408123, 4632567
1	Reddish Brown	4081b	Plate 1 x 1 with Clip Light Type 2	4541285
8	Reddish Brown	3023	Plate 1 x 2	4211150
3	Tan	3023	Plate 1 x 2	4113917
4	White	60470	Plate 1 x 2 with 2 Clips Horizontal	4556152
4	Black	60478	Plate 1 x 2 with Handle on End	4515368
2	Tan	48336	Plate 1 x 2 with Handle Type 2	4217562
1	Dark Bluish Gray	14419	Plate 1 x 2 with Socket Joint-8 with Friction and Ball Joint-8	6039482
1	Dark Bluish Gray	14704	Plate 1 x 2 with Socket Joint-8 with Friction Centre	6146792
4	Black	3794	Plate 1 x 2 without Groove with 1 Centre Stud	379426
1	Reddish Brown	3794	Plate 1 x 2 without Groove with 1 Centre Stud	4219726
3	Reddish Brown	3623	Plate 1 x 3	4211152
2	Tan	3623	Plate 1 x 3	4121921
1	Blue	3710	Plate 1 x 4	371023

Quantity	Color	Element	Element Name	LEGO Number
1	Reddish Brown	3710	Plate 1 x 4	4211190
2	Black	3022	Plate 2 x 2	302226
3	Blue	3022	Plate 2 x 2	302223, 4613973
1	Tan	3022	Plate 2 x 2	4114084
1	Blue	2420	Plate 2 x 2 Corner	242023
2	Reddish Brown	2420	Plate 2 x 2 Corner	4211257
1	Tan	3021	Plate 2 x 3	30215, 4118790
1	Black	3020	Plate 2 x 4	302026
1	Reddish Brown	54200	Slope Brick 31 1 x 1 x 2/3	4260486, 4504376
1	Tan	4286	Slope Brick 33 3 x 1	4248193, 4519898, 6058090
2	Black	15068	Slope Brick Curved 2 x 2 x 0.667	6053077
2	Tan	32064b	Technic Brick 1 x 2 with Axlehole Type 2	4233494
4	Blue	4274	Technic Pin 1/2	4143005
4	Black	62462	Technic Pin Joiner Round with Slot	4526982
6	Black	4697b	Technic Pneumatic T-Piece - Type 2	6104209
4	Black	3070b	Tile 1 x 1 with Groove	307026
1	Light Bluish Gray	3070b	Tile 1 x 1 with Groove	4211415
1	Reddish Brown	3070b	Tile 1 x 1 with Groove	4211288
6	Tan	3070b	Tile 1 x 1 with Groove	4125253
2	Black	3069b	Tile 1 x 2 with Groove	306926
2	Tan	3069b	Tile 1 x 2 with Groove	30695, 4114026
4	Reddish Brown	63864	Tile 1 x 3 with Groove	6100769
1	Tan	63864	Tile 1 x 3 with Groove	6131896
1	Blue	2431	Tile 1 x 4 with Groove	243123
1	White	14719	Tile 2 x 2 Corner	6058329
2	Black	11203	Tile 2 x 2 Inverted with Groove	6013867
2	White	11203	Tile 2 x 2 Inverted with Groove	6013866
2	Blue	3068b	Tile 2 x 2 with Groove	306823
2	White	3068b	Tile 2 x 2 with Groove	306801

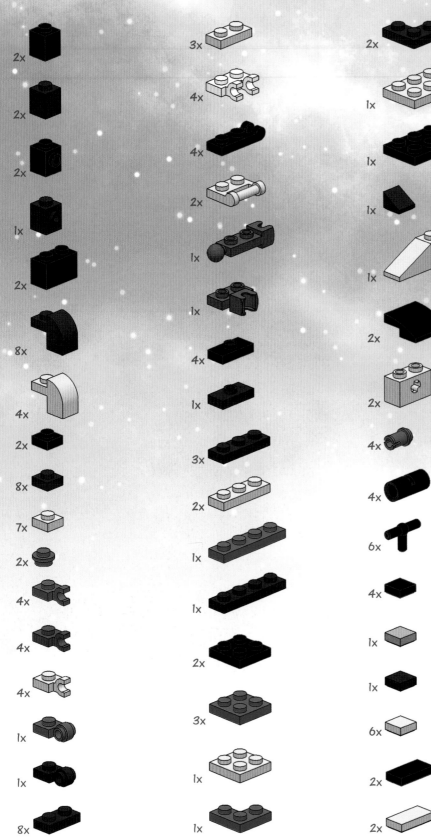

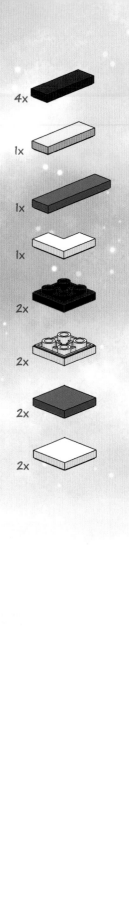

AT—AT

This size of AT-AT results from a special request: I was asked whether I could create one this small, a challenge that turned out to be far from easy. Consequently, I feel entirely justified in presenting the finer details of this model. Looking at the assembly instructions now, I am delighted to have eventually hit upon a version that is so simple to reproduce—even though the project posed considerably difficulties at the outset. Try to work out your own solutions sometimes and just start buildng. You will discover how much fun it can be!

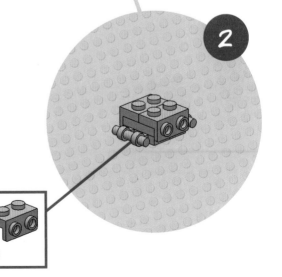

1

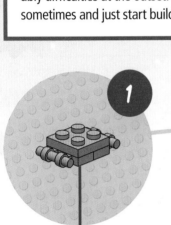

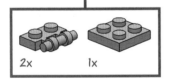

2x   1x

2

2x

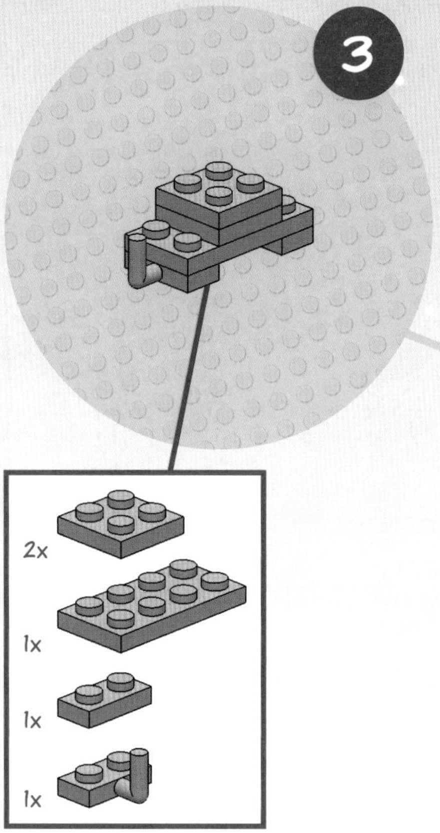

3

2x   1x

2x

1x

1x

1x

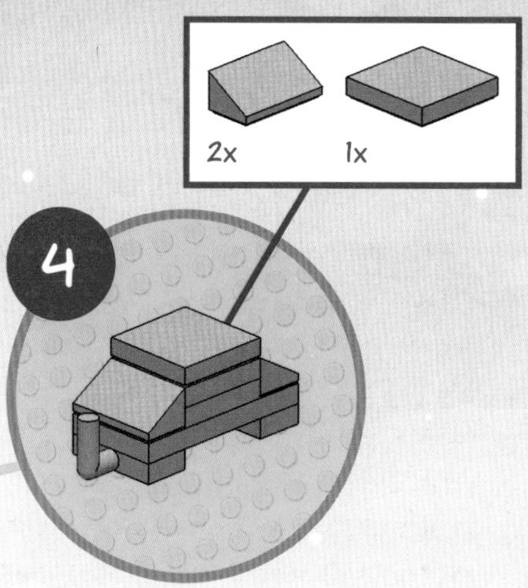

4

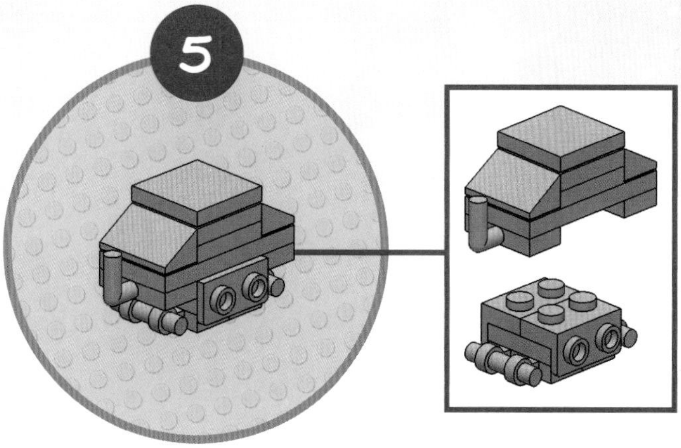

5

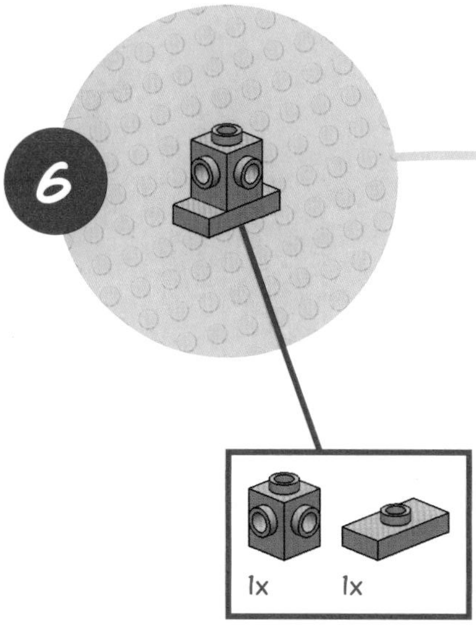

6

1x   1x

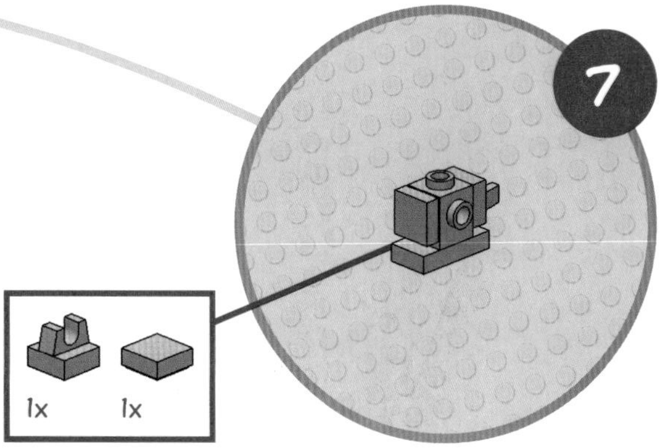

7

1x   1x

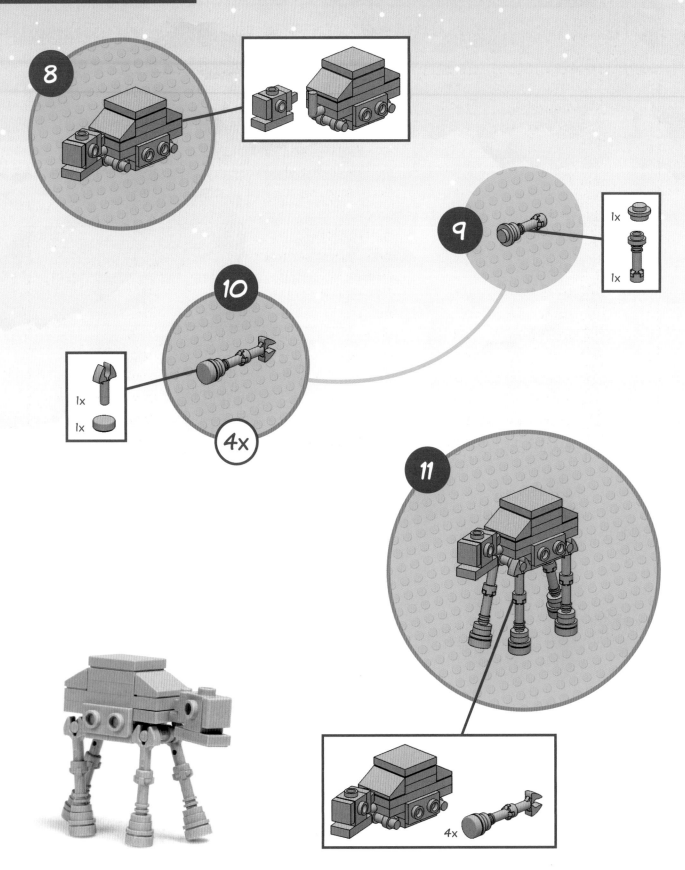

PARTS LIST

Quantity	Color		Element	Element Name	LEGO Number
4		Light Bluish Gray	48729b	Bar 1.5L with Clip	4542590
2		Light Bluish Gray	99781	Bracket 1 x 2 - 1 x 2 Down	4654582
1		Light Bluish Gray	4733	Brick 1 x 1 with Studs on Four Sides	4211511
4		Light Bluish Gray	64567	Minifig Tool Light Sabre Hilt	4212074, 4539481, 4581155
4		Light Bluish Gray	4073	Plate 1 x 1 Round	4211525
1		Light Bluish Gray	3023	Plate 1 x 2	3023194, 4211398
2		Light Bluish Gray	2540	Plate 1 x 2 with Handle	4211632
1		Light Bluish Gray	4623	Plate 1 x 2 with Vertical Bar on Long Side and Long Arm	4211505
1		Light Bluish Gray	3794	Plate 1 x 2 without Groove with 1 Centre Stud	4211451
3		Light Bluish Gray	3022	Plate 2 x 2	4211397
1		Light Bluish Gray	3020	Plate 2 x 4	4211395
2		Light Bluish Gray	85984	Slope Brick 31 1 x 2 x 0.667	4568637
4		Light Bluish Gray	98138	Tile 1 x 1 Round with Groove	4650260
1		Light Bluish Gray	2555	Tile 1 x 1 with Clip	2555194, 4211369, 6030711
1		Light Bluish Gray	3070b	Tile 1 x 1 with Groove	4211415
1		Light Bluish Gray	3068b	Tile 2 x 2 with Groove	4211413

4x

4x

1x

4x

2x

1x

3x

1x

1x

2x

1x

1x

4x

1x

2x

1x

TIE—X1—TURBO STARFIGHTER

I came up with the idea for Darth Vader's TIE-X1-Starfighter over 30 years ago when I saw these wings for the first time. The reason I have only just built it now is because of the printed 1x1 circular tile that appeared in 2015. It immediately occurred to me that this piece would make an excellent front windshield. I was consequently reminded of my original idea and finally brought the project to completion. This was undoubtedly the longest-maturing idea for a model I have ever had.

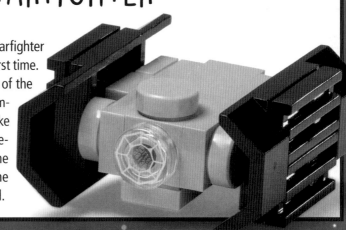

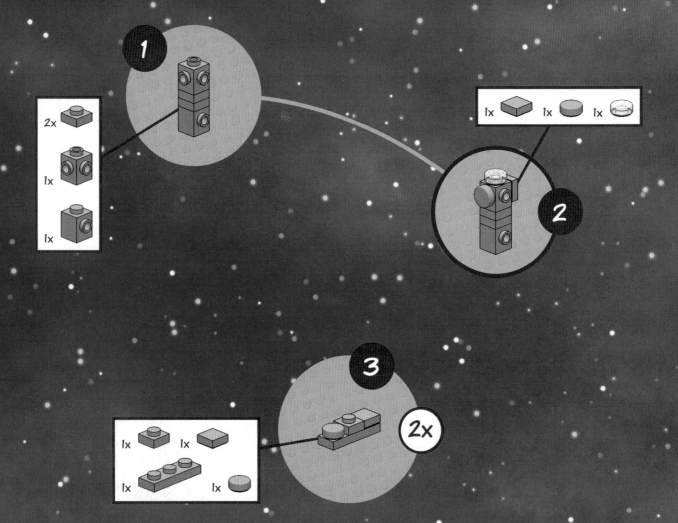

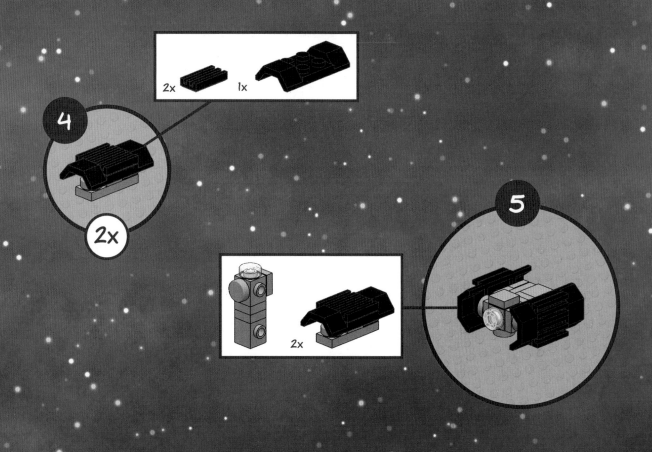

PARTS LIST

Quantity	Color		Element	Element Name	LEGO Number
1		Light Bluish Gray	4733	Brick 1 x 1 with Studs on Four Sides	4211511
1		Light Bluish Gray	47905	Brick 1 x 1 with Studs on Two Opposite Sides	4213567
4		Light Bluish Gray	3024	Plate 1 x 1	4211399
2		Light Bluish Gray	3623	Plate 1 x 3	3623194, 4211429
1		Trans Clear	98138pb024	Tile 1 x 1 Round with Cockpit Pattern	6091590
3		Light Bluish Gray	98138	Tile 1 x 1 Round with Groove	4650260
3		Light Bluish Gray	3070b	Tile 1 x 1 with Groove	4211415
4		Black	2412b	Tile 1 x 2 Grille with Groove	241226
2		Black	3787	Mudguard 2 x 4 without Studs	

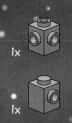

IMPERIAL STAR DESTROYER

The official models of this spacecraft come in a wide range of different sizes. However, this being one of my favorite spaceships of the series, I was keen to develop my very own version of it. Using the cheese grater and hangar entrance and including a Blockade Runner, I have designed a creation of my very own based on very specific personal requirements.

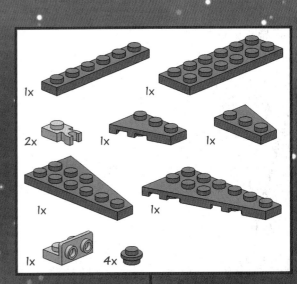

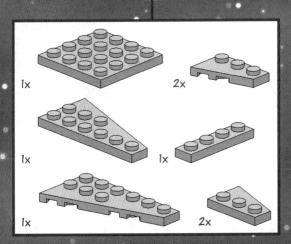

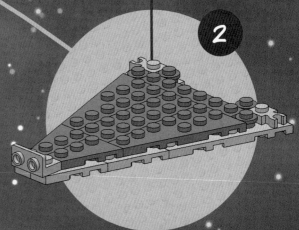

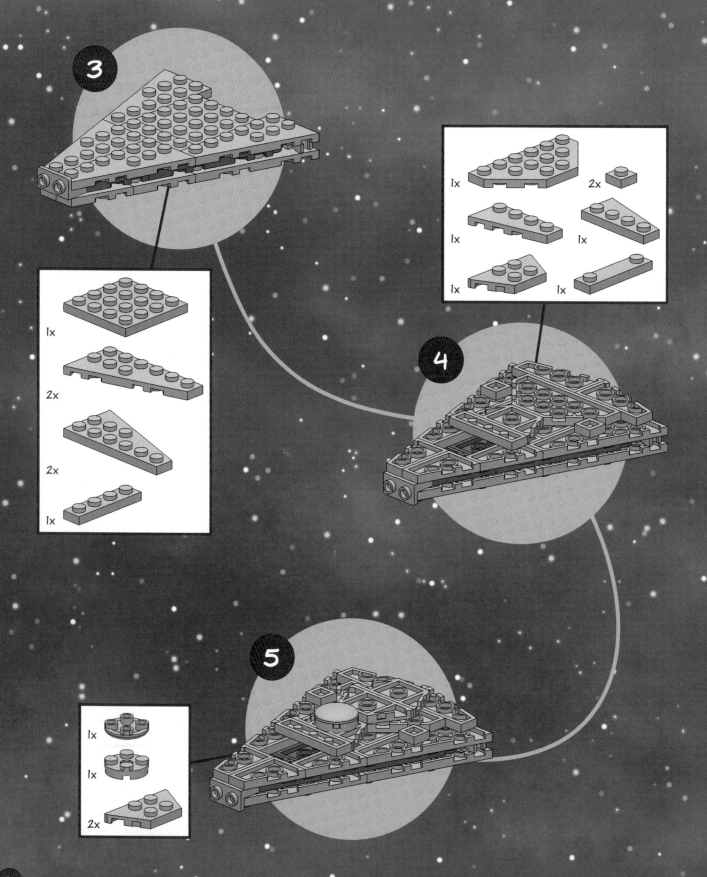

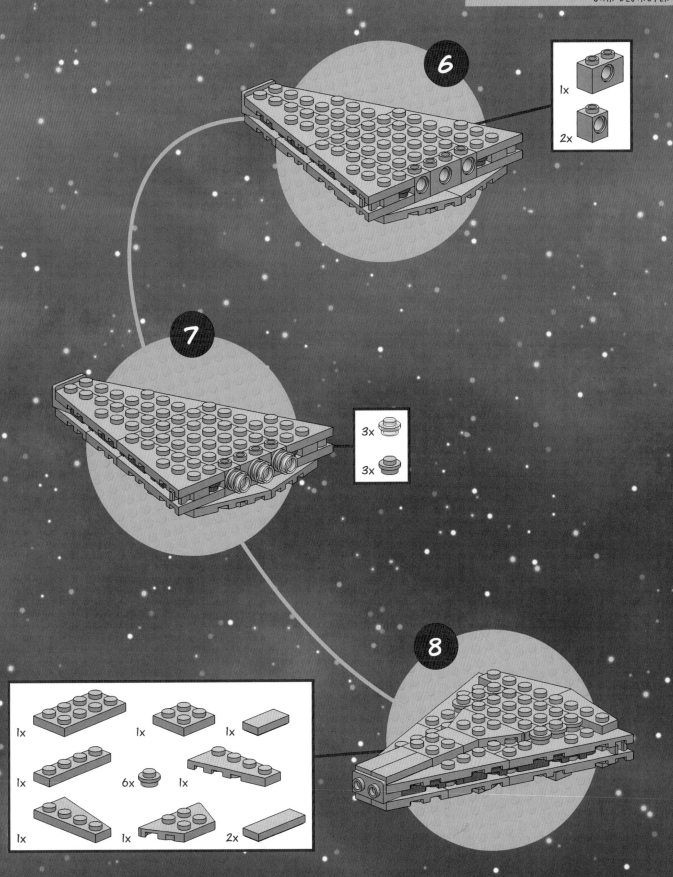

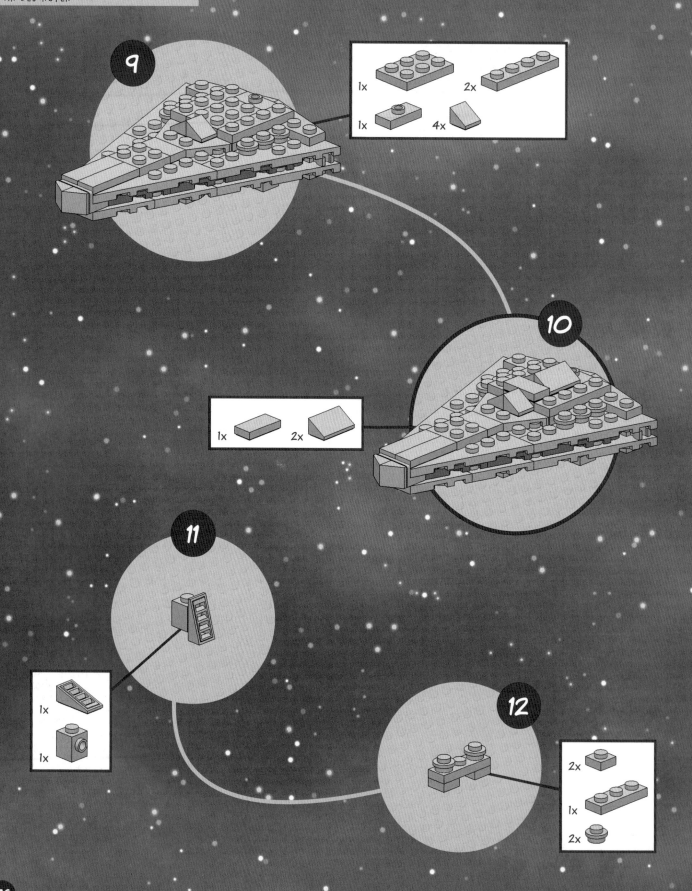

13

14

15

1x 1x 4x

PARTS LIST

Quantity	Color		Element	Element Name	LEGO Number
1		Light Bluish Gray	99780	Bracket 1 x 2 - 1 x 2 Up	6004990
1		Light Bluish Gray	87087	Brick 1 x 1 with Stud on 1 Side	4558953
1		Light Bluish Gray	2654	Dish 2 x 2	4211372, 4278273
4		Light Bluish Gray	3024	Plate 1 x 1	4211399
4		Dark Bluish Gray	4073	Plate 1 x 1 Round	4210633
11		Light Bluish Gray	4073	Plate 1 x 1 Round	4211525
3		Trans Light Blue	4073	Plate 1 x 1 Round	4163917
4		White	4073	Plate 1 x 1 Round	614101
2		Light Bluish Gray	4085c	Plate 1 x 1 with Clip Vertical Type 3	4211479
1		Light Bluish Gray	3794	Plate 1 x 2 without Groove with 1 Centre Stud	4211451
1		White	3794	Plate 1 x 2 without Groove with 1 Centre Stud	379401
1		Light Bluish Gray	3623	Plate 1 x 3	3623194, 4211429
5		Light Bluish Gray	3710	Plate 1 x 4	4211445
1		Light Bluish Gray	92593	Plate 1 x 4 with Two Studs	4599498
1		Dark Bluish Gray	3666	Plate 1 x 6	4211056
1		Light Bluish Gray	3022	Plate 2 x 2	4211397
1		Light Bluish Gray	4032b	Plate 2 x 2 Round with Axlehole Type 2	4211475
1		Light Bluish Gray	3021	Plate 2 x 3	4211396
1		Light Bluish Gray	3020	Plate 2 x 4	4211395
1		Dark Bluish Gray	3795	Plate 2 x 6	4211002
1		Light Bluish Gray	2419	Plate 3 x 6 without Corners	4211352

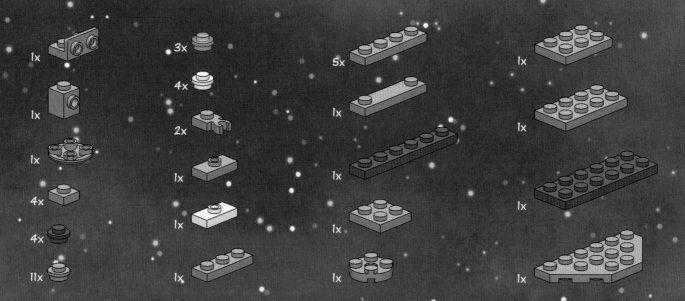

Quantity	Color		Element	Element Name	LEGO Number
2		Light Bluish Gray	3031	Plate 4 x 4	4211403, 4243797
1		Light Bluish Gray	61409	Slope Brick 18 2 x 1 x 2/3 Grille	6092111
4		Light Bluish Gray	54200	Slope Brick 31 1 x 1 x 2/3	4521921
2		Light Bluish Gray	85984	Slope Brick 31 1 x 2 x 0.667	4568637
2		Light Bluish Gray	6541	Technic Brick 1 x 1 with Hole	4211535
1		Light Bluish Gray	3700	Technic Brick 1 x 2 with Hole	4211440
1		White	3070b	Tile 1 x 1 with Groove	307001
2		Light Bluish Gray	3069b	Tile 1 x 2 with Groove	4211414
2		Light Bluish Gray	63864	Tile 1 x 3 with Groove	4558169
1		Dark Bluish Gray	43723	Wing 2 x 3 Left	4210872
2		Light Bluish Gray	43723	Wing 2 x 3 Left	4211794
1		Dark Bluish Gray	43722	Wing 2 x 3 Right	4210869
2		Light Bluish Gray	43722	Wing 2 x 3 Right	4211791
4		Light Bluish Gray	51739	Wing 2 x 4	4252368, 4507056
2		Light Bluish Gray	41770	Wing 2 x 4 Left	4211735
2		Light Bluish Gray	41769	Wing 2 x 4 Right	4211732
1		Dark Bluish Gray	54384	Wing 3 x 6 Left	4290149
3		Light Bluish Gray	54384	Wing 3 x 6 Left	4282789
1		Dark Bluish Gray	54383	Wing 3 x 6 Right	4290150
3		Light Bluish Gray	54383	Wing 3 x 6 Right	4282786

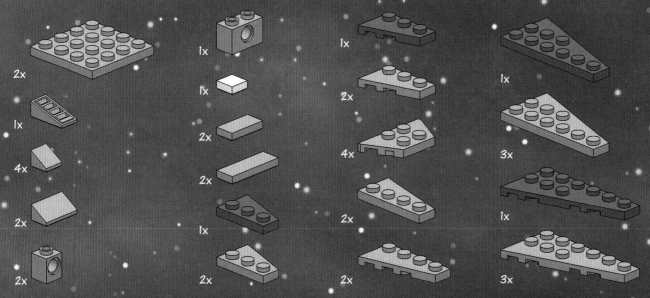

2x   1x   1x   1x

1x   1x   2x   1x

4x   2x   4x   3x

2x   2x   2x   1x

2x   1x   2x   3x

2x   2x   2x   3x

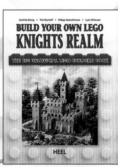

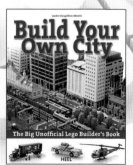